BEATING
THE PROPERTY
CLOCK

If you want to know how...

The Landlord's Guide to Student Letting

How to find an investment property and let it out to students

The Buy to Let Handbook

How to invest for profit in residential property and manage the letting yourself

The Self-Build Survival Guide

How to build or renovate your dream home – the eco-friendly way

The Beginner's Guide to Property Investment

The ultimate handbook for first-time buyers and would-be property investors

howtobooks

for full details, please send for a free copy of the latest catalogue to:
How To Books Ltd, Spring Hill House, Spring Hill Road,
Begbroke, Oxford OX5 1RX United Kingdom

BEATING THE PROPERTY CLOCK

HOW TO UNDERSTAND & EXPLOIT THE PROPERTY CYCLE FOR mAXIMUm GAIN

·REVISED AND UPDATED· 2ND SECOND EDITION·

AJAY AHUJA

howtobooks

Published by
How To Books Ltd
Spring Hill House
Spring Hill Road
Begbroke
Oxford OX5 1RX. United Kingdom
Tel: (01865) 375794. Fax: (01865) 379162
info@howtobooks.co.uk
www.howtobooks.co.uk

First edition 2004
Second edition 2007

British Library Cataloguing in Publication Data
A catalogue record for this book is available from the British Library

Cover design by Baseline Arts Ltd, Oxford
Produced for How To Books by Deer Park Productions, Tavistock
Designed and typeset by Baseline Arts Ltd, Oxford
Printed and bound by Bell & Bain Ltd, Glasgow

NOTE: The material contained in this book is set out in good faith for general guidance and no liability can be accepted for loss or expense incurred as a result of relying in particular circumstances on statements made in this book. The laws and regulations are complex and liable to change, and readers should check the current position with the relevant authorities before making personal arrangements.

Contents

I dedicate this book to my mother

Special thanks to my Hana and my family, Anjana, Tom and Rosa.

I would like to also thank the people with whom I have had many conversations: David Delaney about property investment; Zach Chaudry about how to make a million(!); Mandip about how to collect rent on time; Emily Shah for giving me the idea in the first place; Gavin for his in-depth questioning; Damian for his even more in-depth questioning; Adam for his help with marketing; and Giles and Nikki for their continued belief.

A note from the author

My father was a teacher and my mother was a nurse. They were one of the first lot of immigrants back in the 1960s to come over to plug the employment gap the UK was suffering. My father was from India and my mother was from Trinidad and Tobago. They had learnt that education literally takes you places! Because of their qualifications they were able to escape the poverty trap within their own countries and join the country they believed would be better for them and their future offspring … and boy were they right!

My father met my mother in 1964 and let's just say it was love at first sight. In 1969 my sister was born. I arrived three days after Christmas in 1971. After I was born we moved to a council house in Harlow, Essex, where my father was offered the house at a discounted price of £4,000 if he taught in one of the secondary schools. My mother took a part-time job as a nurse at one of the industrial areas but she always made sure she was there to pick us up from school.

Both my sister and I were encouraged to study and go on to further education and this we both did. My sister went to Imperial College, London, went on to do a PhD is now a journalist for *The Times*. I went to The London School of Economics and then on to train and qualify as a chartered accountant with Deloitte & Touche.

Let me tell you now that my parents were very proud of us. We had pretty much gone beyond their expectations of what they wanted for us. My mother would sing our praises to all her friends that her daughter wrote for the prestigious *Times* newspaper (which is pretty much my sister's dream job) and her son worked for one of the world famous 'Big 6' accountancy firms.

But I couldn't share this feeling my mother had. She would proudly state 'My son is a chartered accountant', but I would struggle to get up in the morning, put my suit on like everyone else, and push the entrance doors below the grand, chrome 'Deloitte & Touche' sign to get in to work. I think my heart sank every morning, Monday to Friday.

I had been on a treadmill of exams after exams. First my GCSEs, then my A levels, then my degree, and then my chartered accountancy exams. All of which I had revised for and passed with flying colours. At age 25 I was considered a success. I had passed the Institute of Chartered Accountants final exams which have a notoriously high failure rate, and I now I was an elite member of this institute with the world at my feet. You would think I should be feeling on top of the world, but the complete opposite was true.

I desperately wished I had failed my exams.

At least then there would have been no expectation of me to progress further in the corporate world. But since I had qualified I had a real chance of rising up the ranks and becoming a senior manager or even a partner. I started to really look at the corporate world as my future as I did not allow myself to see anything else. I was a chartered accountant for heaven's sake. I could really become king of the corporates!

I looked at how the corporate world worked. To rise up the first ranks you needed to be punctual, friendly with the right people and create the right perception of yourself to your seniors. I knew this because I had been told this by my direct bosses. 'There is no room for mavericks Ajay' I was told. My performance would be judged on all the things that I thought were irrelevant. I was not going to be judged on how hard I worked, how much I made the company, or how much effort I put in. I was going to be judged on whether I turned up to work at 9am, whether I stayed beyond 5.30pm with all the other managers and whether I socialised with the right crowd.

I really struggled with this. I just didn't fit in. I couldn't understand why it had to be so. So much so I turned to alcohol. I think having to appear to be this corporate guy took so much effort on my part I needed a release when I got home. This didn't help things! I would start turning up late for work, other staff members would talk about my lateness (it even became an office joke!) and I would want (and often did) to leave at 5.30pm on the dot.

It got to the stage where I was always looking for ways of getting off work early (like delivering files to another office round the corner at 4pm and not coming back) or taking sick days or unannounced holidays.

Then the final blow was dealt. Another colleague of mine who was at the same level as me got promoted and I didn't. It was no surprise. He worked hard and I didn't. I felt embarrassed that I did not get promoted and to save further humiliation, at age 27, I handed in my resignation before they even needed to explain why I didn't get promotion. It was funny. When I did hand in my resignation they said 'We were expecting this!'. They could see I was a maverick and there were no places for mavericks in accountancy, as I had already been told. I'm sure if any of my superiors know of my success today they would say 'I always knew he would be an entrepreneur'.

When I handed in my resignation I had no idea how I was going to provide for myself. All I knew was that I would NEVER work for anyone else ever again. I have to say I was close to suffering depression in the last year of my working career. Money can never be so important that it takes your mental health and wellbeing away from you.

I arranged a £10,000 overdraft before I left work to remain solvent and got the hell out of there! The first three months after leaving work in October 1999 I partied. And I partied hard. I went to Ibiza twice, went out every night and did absolutely nothing to build any kind of future for myself. Looking back, I think I gave myself this time as I felt I deserved it for putting myself through five years of corporate life.

During my drinking days I had built up quite a few friendships but I started to notice something – I was different! I had slightly more intellect than these people I knew and I also used to have creative ideas which when I presented them were dismissed quickly as nonsense. I would come up with ideas on how to make money or do something that would be different from drinking down the pub, but they were swiftly quashed.

It got to a point where I got fed up with my ideas being dismissed, and I quickly saw that these friends were happy where they were. They didn't want change. I realised I was not happy where I was so I made the firm decision that I was going to start afresh. I cut my ties with the group I was drinking with, rented a room in a completely new area and said to myself 'I'm going to make something of myself!'.

This was the best thing I ever did. With hindsight, I realised that the crowd I was hanging about with were preventing me to be who I really wanted to be. I now know the phrase 'Show me your friends and I'll tell you who you are' is so true. This is why I no longer hang out with the corporate gang or the drinking gang but with the entrepreneur's gang! I often find myself discussing ideas with fellow entrepreneurs and we're always trying to change or do things differently. Its never 'No' but often 'How?'. Not 'No, you can't do that' but 'How can you do that?'.

So its now the year 2000 and I'm sitting in my room, while everyone else is at work, thinking – how can I make some money? My overdraft is sitting at around £5,000 with only £5,000 left, I'm burning £1,000 every month so at this rate I'll be bankrupt in five months and I'm going to have to go back to work! Going bankrupt I could deal with but going back to work … NO WAY! The fear of going back to work I have to say was my biggest driver to do something and not the money. I'm not a materialistic person. Even though I can afford better I live the lifestyle of most other people. I live in a 4-bedroom house, I drive an old car and I shop in Tesco's!

Back then in 2000 I realised I was already rich. I was rich with time. I was waking up thinking 'What can I do today?' I realised that working one hour for yourself was like working eight hours for somebody else. This was because I was interested in the work I was doing as I 100% directly benefited from it. Just think about it for one moment. One hour = eight hours. One self-employed hour = eight employed hours. I would work 12 hours a day which equated to 96 employed hours. Its no surprise then that I became successful very quickly. This was because I loved what I was doing.

I started doing everything and anything to make money. Premium rate numbers, people's tax returns, the odd day of subcontracted work for a local accountant, trading cars but also investing in property.

At the time I didn't know my property investments would be as successful as they were. It was just one of those activities I was doing as well as the other stuff. I had four properties in 2000. You see whilst my work colleagues were renting flashy apartments and burning their salary on rent, I was living in a shared house, saving up my salary for deposits and buying properties back in my home town. I had my own house in Harlow which I had bought and lived in, then briefly rented out, and three other buy to lets in Harlow rented out.

One of the key tools I found important to me was the internet. I used it at work to collect emails and search for cars to buy! I got a dial up connection installed in my room and I would use this connection to research potential money making ideas. It was at this point I stumbled across a site called rightmove.co.uk.

Rightmove were great. Instead of searching each estate agent's database for their properties Rightmove aggregated all the estate agents databases so you could perform one search. I was used to paying £35,000 for a 1-bedroom flat in Harlow back in 2000. So I would search for properties in Harlow for less than £50,000 and see what came up. I had this formula that if it would rent out on a month-by-month basis for 1% of the purchase price then I would buy it. So if it was for £50,000 and it would rent out for £500 or more, I would buy it. I would see a deal like this once every other week. It was safe to say Harlow wasn't overflowing with these properties which I thought were great deals.

I then asked myself the question why don't I invest further afield? So when I searched on Rightmove I put the distance parameter at a 40 mile radius of Harlow and then pressed 'search'. I have to say this was a turning point in my life. Remember here that I had been used to paying £35,000 for a 1-bedroom flat and these were hard to come by.

The first property that came up was a 5-bedroom, three storey house for £20,000! I thought this price must be a misprint, but then I saw next to this on the list a 3-bedroom house for £23,500 in the same area. So I rang up, spoke to someone about it and asked it if was for real and not a misprint. They confirmed that it was for real but the property had gone. I asked about rents and they all fitted my criteria of being greater than 1% of the purchase price. I had to take a trip to this 'hotspot'. This hotspot was called Corby in Northamptonshire.

I went up there and met with the three estate agents there and was treated like a king. They had actually found someone who wanted to buy these properties in these deprived areas. I would be shown round these properties, all with price tags under £30,000. It really was a buyer's market. My problem was there were too many properties and I didn't have enough cash! I liken these days to being a kid in a sweetie shop with only 50p in your pocket. I wanted every sweet but couldn't afford it.

What I did next makes me still wince when I think about it. From my bedroom I made literally thousands of applications for unsecured finance, credit cards, overdrafts and other sources of finance. Most said 'no' but some actually said 'yes'. I raised £100,000 of unsecured finance, £15,000 on credit cards and £40,000 by remortgaging my then current portfolio of four properties and bought as much as I could.

I bought flats, houses and town houses. They all fitted the 1% rule (now known as a 12% yield) and some even fitted a 2% rule, meaning that the properties yielded 24%.

But then something even more strange started to happen. I thought I was the only person doing this in Corby, but other people started emerging. The prices started to be pushed up. But it didn't happen over months, it happened over weeks! So stuff that I had agreed to buy had gone up by 50% by the time I had completed. But I would go straight for a remortgage after I completed. You would then get the absurd happening. I would buy something for say £20,000, in three months I would complete on it, and then get it remortgaged at £40,000, with a further £15,000 out of which I would buy three more properties.

I didn't stop at Corby. I bought everywhere that fitted my 1% criteria. The closer the better. But I found that I was getting priced out. So I would just travel further north to get the properties that yielded 12%. And all the time growing in wealth as everything I was buying was rising rapidly.

I used to manage my properties myself. I would go, all 5ft 4" of me, to the roughest parts of town to collect rent from junkies, drug dealers and the serial unemployed! It still amazes me that I did that back then. But my mother was becoming extremely worried, so I took on someone who handled it for me from then on. I had 20 properties in all by 2001.

I then decided it was time to move out of my rented room and get myself a nice little pad. I bought a 3-bedroom detached house in Romford, Essex, for £132,000 and lived there while still buying up in and around the East Midlands and Essex. It was while living in this house that I had the idea to tell people about what I was doing. It was so easy – I wanted to tell other people about what I was doing and say 'Hey – you can do this!'.

I wrote my first book, *The Buy to Let Bible*, and that is my bestseller. It has sold over 100,000 copies nationwide and is available in every book store including Tesco's! I have since written nine more books on property investment and escaping the rat race. I'd like to think I have helped people realise their financial dreams and have given them back precious time that you can never get back once its gone.

Since 2002 I have moved to a 4-bedroom house with my girlfriend Hana who really looks after me so I can further my pursuits in property investing, property sourcing and internet businesses.

We have no children (yet!) but I have one niece, Rosa, whom I adore, and I fit into *her* life – not the other way round.

My current portfolio currently stands at £11.3m and has £1.7m worth of properties in the pipeline waiting to be added. I aim to buy one property a week over the next few years or so. I'm currently investing in Scotland, Derbyshire and Lincolnshire.

So why am I telling you all this? Well, I suppose I want to let you know it is possible to be your own boss. I'm a regular guy that wants pretty much the same as anyone else. I want to be in control of my life and I want to have an okay life. I want to be rich with my time, to have material goods that make my life comfortable and I want to build positive relationships with the people around me.

But I want you to know this: I do not possess any special characteristics compared to anyone else and neither do I consider myself as lucky. All I did was apply myself to do something that I wanted to do. This was to become financially free from an employer. I believe ANYONE can do this with the right attitude.

I wish you luck with your investments.

Ajay Ahuja

CHAPTER ONE

The Property Clock

The cyclical pattern

Property prices follow a cyclical pattern. Property prices rise and then property prices fall. The reasons why will become apparent further on, but for some reason they do rise and then fall. So what is the best time for an investor to become interested? When the prices start to rise, of course!

If we were to speed up this process over a notional 12-hour period, with 12 noon being the point when they first rise and 6 o'clock being the point when they first start to fall, then we would have the following diagram:

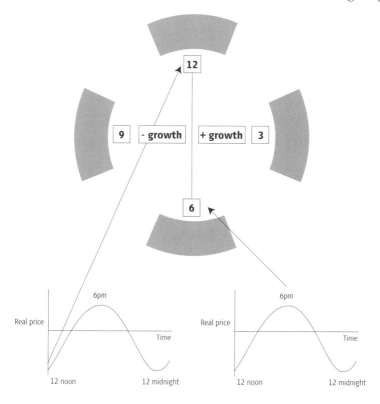

At 12 noon prices increase until 6pm and then they start to fall. We can see that anyone who has any sense gets interested anywhere between 12 noon and 6pm. So who buys between 12 noon and 6pm? Everyone! Who is everyone and why do they buy? The following people buy exclusively and their reasons are as follows.

Buyers	Why?
Professional property investors	A professional property investor will buy a property which will enable them to buy other properties and put money in their pocket. It will enable them to benefit from capital growth so that they can remortgage and buy further properties, and when rented out it will, after voids, letting agent's fees, tax and other expenses, provide a positive cashflow.
Novice/speculative investors	A novice/speculative investor will invest in a growth area because they will believe that the trend upwards in price will continue. They are less concerned in fundamentals as they are not aware of the fundamentals – they simply believe that the trend is upwards.
Owner-occupiers	The owner-occupier will buy because if they delay buying it will cost them more. So it is in their interest to buy sooner rather than later as their overall purchase price will be higher the longer they leave it.

So who buys between 6pm and 12 midnight? Prices are falling now so the novice/speculative investor becomes uninterested as there are no capital growth prospects and the owner-occupier will wait until the prices drop further. The only buyer remaining is the professional investor.

Buyers	Why?
Professional property investors	The only time a professional property investor will buy in this market is if the investment puts money in their pocket. They will invest in a falling market due to the property market providing a better return on their other investments such as the stock market, other businesses or a bank or building society. It is the professional property investor who prevents the property market falling to nothing. It is the professional investor who provides the cushion to the fall.

Based on the table above we can see that:

■ The professional investor buys on known information i.e. the property purchase puts money in their pocket.

■ The novice/speculative investor and owner-occupier buy based only on the fact that the trend of prices is rising.

So how does the professional investor estimate whether a property will put money in their pocket? It's called **gross yield**. Gross yield, in mathematical terms, is:

$$\frac{\text{Annual rent x 100 (\%)}}{\text{Property purchase price}}$$

Now annual rent is a pretty static figure. Rents do not rise and then fall. They simply rise slowly and steadily the same way wages do. So in real terms they remain the same. However, property prices are far more volatile. Property prices gather momentum far in excess of the rate of wage inflation and hence rise and fall at a greater rate than the rate of inflation – but we will get to that later.

Assuming we agree with the stability of rental prices and the volatility of property prices, we can show that:

Property prices are inversely related to yield

That is to say that as property prices rise the yield falls. Let me show you this example:

$$\frac{\text{Annual rent: £10,000}}{\text{Property price: £100,000}}$$

Yield is then:

$$\frac{£10,000}{£100,000} \times 100 = 10\%$$

Now let's say that property prices increase to £110,000 in six months. A professional investor considering the market will now consider the yield to be:

$$\frac{£10,000}{£110,000} \times 100 = 9.1\%$$

So we can see that as the property price increases from £100,000 to £110,000 the yield decreases from 10% to 9.1%.

Using this same example let's say that property prices fall from £100,000 to £90,000 in six months. A professional investor considering the market will now consider the yield to be:

$$\frac{£10,000}{£90,000} = 11.1\%$$

So we can see that as the property price decreases from £100,000 to £90,000 the yield increases from 10% to 11.1%.

This is called an **inverse relationship** as the yield and property price move in different directions. So if we were to create a **yield vs time** graph then it would be the exact opposite of the **real price vs time** graph.

Fitting the yield curves into the clock it will look like this:

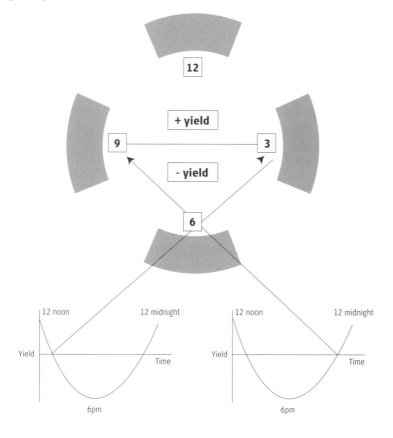

When you should invest

So if you're a sensible investor then you will invest during the periods 12 noon to 3pm, and 9pm to 12 midnight. This is because, as with any investment you make, you will make money as the investment puts money in your pocket because it's a positive yield.

If we superimpose these two strategies then we come up with the face of the property clock:

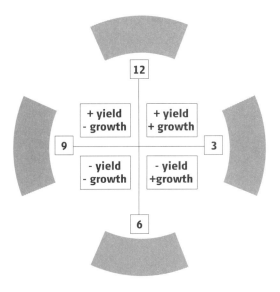

What pushes the clock round

But every clock needs power to move. I call this power the **drivers.** The clock hands need power to take them round the clock. So what moves the clock hands round?

The following drivers push the property clock round with regularity:

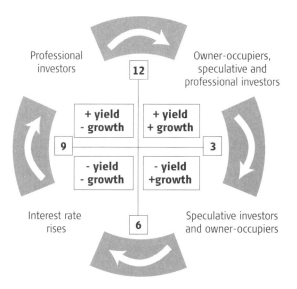

So we can see that:

■ everybody drives the price from 12 noon to 3pm;

■ speculative investors and owner-occupiers *only* drive the prices from 3pm to 6pm;

■ interest rate rises then drive the price downwards from 6pm to 9pm;

■ professional investors drive the price downwards even further from 9pm to 12 midnight but prevent the prices from falling to zero.

The clock quarter regions (being 12 noon-3pm, 3pm-6pm, 6pm-9pm and 9pm-12 midnight) can be named quite specifically as:

Clock quarter	Name
12 noon – 3pm	Hot spot
3pm – 6pm	Cooling spot
6pm – 9pm	Cold spot
9pm – 12 midnight	Warm spot

The reasons why they are so named will be explained later. However, we now have the complete face, drivers and names for each clock quarter for the property clock:

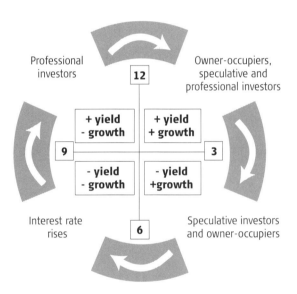

This clock is relevant to any property market that exists within the following conditions:

1. Variable interest rate environment
2. Easily obtainable buy-to-let mortgage environment
3. Lack of long-term fixed interest rate mortgage (typically greater than ten years) environment.

The UK market fits this model. If any of these conditions is eliminated then the clock slows down. If all conditions are eliminated then the clock STOPS! Assuming that none of these things happens then the strategy is:

a) Know when the clock strikes 12 noon most importantly and
b) Know when the clock strikes 3pm, 6pm and 9pm.

In the rest of this book I am going to ignore wage inflation. Even though a house costs twice as much in 20 years you can be sure that you will be earning twice as much. I am going to assume real prices. This makes the figures simple. Actual prices rise and fall but real prices remain the same.

CHAPTER TWO
Growth

Calculating growth

There are many investors who invest in property solely for the growth. They are not concerned with making a rental profit (sometimes happy to make a rental loss!) but with making an above average gain on their initial investment. Annual capital growth (ACG) can be determined by:

Current market value one year after purchase (**CMV1**) - **purchase price (PP) = annual capital growth (AGC1)**

Basically it's how much your property has gone up by in a year of ownership. For future years ACG is:

$$CMVn - CMVn\text{-}1 = ACGn$$

In simple terms it's the difference between the value of the property now and one year ago.

Understanding +/- growth

Understanding why property prices rise and then fall is very important if we want to make money! It is property prices that drive yield, not the other way round, hence what affects property prices is everything. Property prices are volatile and rents are stable. Experts call the rise and fall in property prices the **boom-bust cycle**. The boom-bust cycle will be directly related to:

1. The general economy and
2. Land values.

This is because property is:

1. *built* on land, and
2. *bought* with money.

So a full understanding of the limited nature of land and the dynamics of the economy will enable you to see where we are in relation to the boom-bust cycle.

Certain principles need to be explained before we enter the boom-bust cycle.

Principle	Description
Land is in limited supply	No matter what we do there is nothing to increase the supply of land more than the surface area of the UK. Undeveloped land belongs predominantly to the aristocracy or local councils. The 'super rich' land owners such as earls, barons and dukes own land that they have inherited from their ancestors. Local councils own land that was passed down through the Magna Carta in 1066. London is not going to get any bigger. What we have is what we've got. Due to this fact it will always attract the speculator. Massive profits can be made by simply holding on to a piece of land and holding out until the surrounding land gets developed.

Principle	Description
The population is growing	A growing population means that there are more ideas, inventions and businesses, hence more is produced which causes a pressure on land requirements to locate all the people and their businesses. Overall land values have to increase.
Increase in land values causes an increase in development of land sites	A land owner will happily hold on to a piece of land as there is no cost to them to do so. If land values rise due to the overall state of the economy rising then they will be tempted to sell. Then either the land owner sells, at a profit, to a developer who then develops on the land or the land owner decides to develop it themselves.
An increase in development of land causes an increase in infrastructure	As development occurs more services are required for the developed areas such as train stations, better road links, schools etc. This causes the overall land values to increase further.
Due to the rise in land values saving increases	Considering that money can only be spent or reinvested the general public become attracted to the returns to be had from property developments and hence they save. This results in people spending less on the high street and hence consumption falls.

Principle	Description
The fall in consumption is hidden by the feel-good factor	Because home owners have experienced an increase in the value of their home they use this security to borrow and spend it on the high street. This increase in borrowing to spend is greater than the amount saved to invest (mentioned above) thus overall consumption increases.
A trade deficit occurs as a result of the rise of consumption	Imports exceed exports to cope with the rate of consumption. This causes a deficit and hence the government must raise rates to attract outside investment to finance the deficit.
As rates rise the returns from property look less attractive	The whole boom is due to property looking attractive to speculative investors because of capital growth. If rates rise property price growth stabilises and thus expected growth is no longer factored into the overall return.

If the availability of land was not restricted then real prices would fluctuate like this:

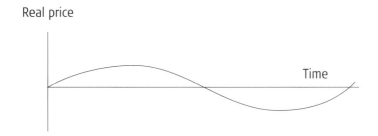

However, the availability of land to be developed is restricted due to speculation, thus prices fluctuate like this:

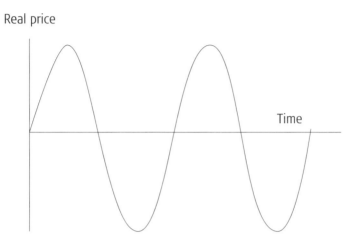

You can see that real prices rise and fall to a greater degree and over a shorter period of time.

The start of the boom

So let's start at when everything is at a sensible price. There are no rapid increases or decreases in prices, supply equals demand and so prices are stable. As the population is growing so is the demand by businesses and individuals to buy commercial and residential property. This means that:

■ properties are either knocked down and built even higher (i.e. the number of floors) to accommodate the increase in demand;

■ properties are built in the undeveloped areas to cope with the increased demand;

■ infrastructure increases to cope with the increase in population.

This is what is supposed to happen but invariably doesn't! Certain land owners do not develop and hold out for even greater increases in value. This in turn causes:

- Developments in areas out of the city centre that put a strain on the infrastructure, e.g. if one can only build in a small town near a city then the road connecting the village to the city centre has to be upgraded and the construction of a train station in the burgeoning village is imminent.

- Undeveloped land in the city centre then becomes even more valuable because of the increased infrastructure surrounding the city centre, thus creating a vicious cycle of surrounding villages becoming over-developed and undeveloped land within the centre being worth potentially millions. Look at city centres with affluent villages/towns surrounding them but with under-developed budget car parks within them being worth a fortune.

- Commercial and residential property within the city centre becoming over-enhanced, i.e. knocked down and built again to a high spec (e.g. skyscraper) which costs a fortune to the investor but with the hope of an even bigger return.

- Developers buying sub-prime land to develop a long way in the future, thus bypassing greedy land owners with high prices on prime plots. However, this money, invested by the developer, is removed from the economy.

So in all, due to the limited supply of land, rising prices being seen by everyone and the number of property programmes or friends' stories of how they made a small fortune, it's only a matter of time before the property speculator emerges. The speculator assumes that you can buy a property, do nothing and sell it in a year and make more than the average annual salary!

Middle of the boom

Due to the introduction of the speculator, who is really only a novice investor, property prices are over-predicted. This means that:

■ existing buildings can be sold to them at inflated prices; or

■ plots of land sold to developers (who are speculators also) are re-sold with the newly built properties to other speculators; in effect the speculator sells to other speculators

because the speculator's view is that the property's value is heading in only one direction – UP!

As prices rise artificially high it encourages even more to be spent on them to gain a higher profit. This results in people saving more, to invest in property, and thus spending less on the high street, lowering overall consumption. However, this is masked temporarily by what's known as the feel-good factor.

Due to some home owners feeling 'richer' they spend on the high street by obtaining unsecured debt such as credit cards or loans. They know that the increase in the value of their home can be accessed, by remortgaging, if they struggle to meet the debt. I'm sure we've all seen the newspaper and TV ads that dominate the advertising spaces offering all types of secured lending. So consumption is maintained by credit provided by the banks.

Towards the end of the boom

As consumption is now fuelled by over-borrowing, it increases to an all-time high. This causes a trade deficit to occur. This is because:

■ Due to people saving to invest in property, money is taken out of the domestic economy and the production of goods at home naturally falls. Importation of goods from abroad is the only way we can satisfy the increase in consumption.

■ To also satisfy the increase in consumption we have to export less to further meet consumer demand.

So we end up importing more than we export thus creating a trade deficit. A trade deficit is where imports exceed exports. That is to say we buy more from abroad than we produce at home. As a result the government cannot raise enough revenue through taxes due to companies not producing enough to tax so the government has to borrow to pay for its spending. The only people who are willing to lend will be from abroad. To attract investors from abroad the government gilt rate has to be increased. This means raising gilt rates so that overseas investors will be attracted which ultimately results in rising interest rates.

At the peak
The peak is not a pretty place! The following misunderstandings and interpretations are occurring:

■ Investments are being made by speculators who are basing their returns on historical growth. Fundamental principles have gone out of the window and investment decisions are being based on previous (and successful) speculative trades and success stories of other investors.

■ Consumption is being fuelled by credit cards and second charge secured loans by home owners feeling good and the reluctance of the consumer to save due to continued increases in their property values.

■ Lenders are lending on perceived equity to home owners which are only a result of speculation.

■ Investing, consuming, lending and borrowing are in excess.

■ Interest rates are rising to cope with the trade deficit, consumer price inflation and to attract people back to saving.

The crash

Something has to cause the crash. Crashes do not happen overnight but they do happen a lot quicker than a boom. Think of a roller-coaster. You know that bit where you hiked up by the machinery to the top of the slope, you can hear the clunking, you get to the top, the clunking stops, you think the cart will rest at the top but it just tips over the edge…

At the top of the slope only the following can and will happen and at a greater pace than the climb:

- Interest rate rises are increased to hurt! They are set to control inflation as we have been spending too much on the high street.

- With the increased interest rate the projected positive cashflows fall. This lowers the overall return on uncompleted capital intensive projects such as the erection of skyscrapers or new builds of luxury apartments.

- The calculation of possible investments now includes the higher rate of interest and now no longer looks so attractive.

- The property development market slows…

If all this speculation had been done with private money then we wouldn't care. The problem is that it's been done with other people's money i.e. the bank's! It's the pulling of the plug by the bank that causes the rapid decline in property investment. Let me show you by a clear chain of reactions:

The projected returns to be made from major property investments have factored-in growth. Monies lent by the bank based on the growth look risky now as the interest rate increases have killed both the growth and the net yield.

The banks get scared and restrict lending. This means that fewer people are able to buy.

Due to fewer people being able to buy land and property because of the restriction by the banks – land and property prices have to fall.

People that have bought at the peak are now facing negative equity. Their debt is greater than the value of their home.

The credit boom cools. Lenders now know that the consumer's property value has fallen hence there is no security to raise finance to clear the lender's debt. Lenders stop lending on an unsecured or a 2nd charge security basis.

Due to higher than expected interest rate rises some borrowers start to default. The lenders try to access the security by issuing repossession orders but due to property prices falling the security simply isn't there. The banks start to lose.

Due to the banks not lending then investment in land and property falls AND consumption falls due to the bank not providing credit to fuel consumption.

Large property development projects predicted in the past to guarantee a profit now look unprofitable due to the lack of buyers, which is the result of the banks not lending. Even renting those developments that have been built looks unprofitable due to higher than anticipated interest rate.

Projects are aborted. They now know that if they carry on they will certainly lose money due to the over-speculation. Exit losses are necessary for damage limitation purposes only.

The mass exit from the property market, heavy bank losses and depressed high street spending causes unemployment.

The feel good factor is non-existent! Borrowing and spending both decline.

The demand for goods on the high street falls. Speculation on the property market also looks poor. People think it's better to save rather than spend.

As property prices fall the potential buyers wait till they bottom out hoping to get a bargain.

Property prices rapidly decline until the professional investor cushions the fall and becomes interested again.

Source: www.landvaluetax.org

This is why property prices move up and down as explained in Chapter 1. Looking at the graph:

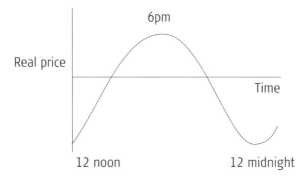

12 noon being the beginning of the boom and 6pm being the beginning of the bust. I really want you to understand this boom-bust cycle. It is the understanding of these fundamentals which will ensure that you never lose in property investment. Please re-read this chapter as many times as it takes so you understand how the boom-bust cycle works. Once you've understood this then we can move on to understanding yield, which is the ultimate tool for any serious property investor.

CHAPTER THREE

Yield

Calculating yield

So how does a professional investor know that a property purchase is going to put money in their pocket? It's called **yield**. Yield is defined as:

> *What you get out relative to what you put in.*

Let's look at this in more detail. Yield really has only two key variables:

1. What you get out.
2. What you put in.

So to calculate yield you simply divide what you get out by what you put in and express it as a percentage. In mathematical terms:

$$\frac{\text{What you get out}}{\text{What you put in}} \times 100 \ (\%)$$

1. What you get out of the property

Can you guess what you get from a property? Well I'll help you – RENT! This is the only thing you can be assured of getting from a property with any real certainty. We're not facing an undersupply of housing in the UK so it is safe to assume that you can expect a steady stream of cash, in the form of rent, as a direct result of owning a property.

Capital growth you can never be sure of. So NEVER factor it in to your calculations as its impossible to calculate! Professional property investors do invest for capital growth, that's for sure, but there is no point factoring it in to your calculations as it can only ever be a predicted figure. Incorporating predictions introduces errors in to the calculations and I hate errors!

So the output for a professional investor is:

What you get out	Term	Definition
Annual rent – annual interest cost – expenses – tax	**Annual rent**	This is the amount of money you can expect to receive from renting out your property. Any other money received from the tenant such as electricity or gas bills is excluded as these receipts should just be covering the cost of the bills anyway. You assume a full 12 month rent without void. Voids are factored in as an expense below.
	Annual interest cost	This is the amount of money you will expect to pay in interest costs as a result of making the property purchase. You do not include any of the repayment part of the cost as this is not a cost. To calculate the annual cost you simply multiply the amount you need to borrow to buy the property by the interest rate being offered by the lender.
	Expenses	Typical expenses will be: **Service charges and ground rent** – This is applicable to leasehold flats in England and Wales. Under the

terms of any long lease in England and Wales you have to pay ground rent (usually never more than £500 per year) and then a maintenance charge called a service charge to cover such things as gardening, repairs, insurance and management of the block.

Look into these service charges as they vary widely. I have two similar flats in differing parts of the country where one charges £5 a month and the other charges £90 a month service charges. Not knowing the potential service charges can result in you making an unexpected loss after all other costs are deducted.

Insurances – You may want all or some of the following insurances: Building, Contents, Rent Guarantee, Boiler, Plumbing and Electric Insurances. Whatever you decide to go for get quotes so you know what these insurances cost and you can factor them in. Some areas can be expensive to insure without you realising it. This could be due to historic flooding, common subsidence or regular burglaries.

Letting agent fees – If you're going to use the services of a letting agent get a breakdown of their fees. Ring them up and ask them to send you their fees list. Be very careful – do not go with the agent with the lowest headline rate. They have hidden costs such as marketing fees, tenancy renewal fees, inventory fees and whatever fees they can come up with! Try to get an idea of total costs for a year's letting.

Repairs – This has to be an estimate. I would tend to over estimate to ensure you don't get caught out. Repairs do even out over time so try to factor in replacement of boilers, carpets, kitchens etc. and then annualise these total costs. £1,000 a year is a good figure to start off with … unless you are thinking of letting out a 10 bedroomed mansion!

Void periods and bad debts – Sometimes tenants do not pay the rent! You have to factor in tenants losing their job, deciding not to pay or absconding. If you've got insurance then this does not have to be factored in as it's covered by the insurance.

One thing insurances cannot cover you for is voids. So it is prudent to allow 1 to 2 months for remarketing and finding the right tenant for the property.

Admin costs – This is usually a small amount but you have to factor in property licences, postage, paper, phone, computer and whatever costs you incur administering your portfolio.

Other costs – This will be specific to the property. If you're thinking of buying a riverside apartment in the city and renting it out to city professionals then your advertising costs may be that little bit higher than a studio flat up north!

Now taking all of the above in to consideration you should come up with a figure. Hopefully this should be a positive figure as this will mean it's potentially profitable. If it isn't then stay away! Don't try to tweak it to make it positive. You'll find your initial figures will be closer to the true figure rather than your recalculated figures trying to make it work.

Tax

Unless you live in a tax haven such as Jersey or Monaco you will have to pay tax. You need to be aware of the following when determining how much taxable profit you have made for the Inland Revenue to tax:

Allowable expenditure – Some expenses are disallowable when it comes to tax. This means you cannot charge these expenses against your profit. The Inland Revenue have this rule about expenses: expenses have to be incurred necessarily, wholly and exclusively to the business for them to be fully deductible against your taxable profits.

If expenses are not allowable then they may be partially allowable, such as mobile phone charges and the use of a private car.

Allowable reliefs – You will be entitled to 'non-cash' expenses called reliefs where they allow a percentage of costs or income to be charged against your taxable profit. Reliefs include Wear and Tear Allowances and Capital Allowances.

Basic or Higher rate tax payer – if you are a higher rate tax payer then you are taxed at 40% compared to 20% for a basic rate tax payer. This will mean a reduced net profit after tax figure. There is an argument that if you were a higher rate tax payer it could be more beneficial for you to invest in other tax friendly investments such as VCTs (Venture Capital Trusts). I do not agree with this as I think property investments are an essential part of anyone's investment portfolio, but you have to consider all points.

ISAs and pension investments can look attractive as they have so many tax benefits but the ISA allowances are very small and the pension benefits seem too far away where the benefits may never be realised. However, look at the yields of these investments and compare them to property. This should steer you towards property!

What you get out should only ever be assessed by what you put in. So let's look at what you put in.

2. What you put in

There can only ever be two sources available to buy properties – your money and borrowed money. Decide which one of the three types of investors you are, then decide which yield calculation is applicable to you.

Look at the following table.

Investor	What you put in	Your money	Borrowed money	Description
High risk investor	Nil	None	Purchase price + Acquisition costs = Total cost of investment	This investor is either a future multi-millionaire or the one that goes bust big style! The return on their cash is infinity as the investor had nothing in the first place. If they pull it off they would have made money out of nothing. This is what I did 10 years ago. I put virtually nothing into my property business and I've got a whole lot out. Yield is very important here as you need rent to cover the costs of borrowing over the whole investment. If you do follow this strategy be very careful and do your maths before you do the buying!

Investor	What you put in	Your money	Borrowed money	Description
Medium risk investor	Some	Deposit + Acquisition costs	Purchase price – Deposit = Mortgage	This is the normal way people invest in property. You put a bit in and the bank puts the rest in. You can get a better return the less you put in IF the market goes your way. Yield is still important as it needs to cover your borrowing costs. The more you put down the less you have to rely on yield.
Low risk investor	All	Purchase price + Acquisition costs	None	This type of investor would be typically looking for a return greater than their bank is offering. They would have used all their money in the bank, forgone the interest they would have earned from the bank and hoped for a return greater than the bank's in the form of capital growth and rents received.

So to calculate yield, as mentioned above, you simply divide what you get out by what you put in and express it as a percentage:

$$\frac{\text{What you get out}}{\text{What you put in}} \times 100\%$$

So the magic calculations that need to be computed, based on what you put in and get out detailed above, are:

Investor	Calculation	Description
High risk investor	$$\frac{(\text{Annual rent} - \text{Annual mortgage cost} - \text{Annual loan cost} - \text{Expenses} - \text{Tax}) \times 100}{(\text{Deposit} + \text{Acquisition costs})}$$	Even though you borrowed everything you still need to see if you're getting a return relative to some basis figure. I consider the unsecured loan taken out to pay for the deposit and acquisition costs as a good basis. The money that's come in will take into account the interest costs of the unsecured loan. Therefore you can get a yield calculation based on what you got out based on what you *theoretically* put in.
Medium risk investor	$$\frac{(\text{Annual rent} - \text{Annual mortgage cost} - \text{Expenses} - \text{Tax}) \times 100}{(\text{Deposit} + \text{Acquisition costs})}$$	Unlike the high risk investor there is no unsecured loan to service so there is no interest cost on the unsecured loan taken off what you get out from the property. You then need to compare this calculated yield to alternative investments.

Investor	Calculation	Description
Low risk investor	$$\frac{(\text{Annual rent} - \text{Expenses} - \text{Tax}) \times 100}{(\text{Property purchase price} + \text{Acquisition costs})}$$	Unlike both investors above there is no borrowing cost as there are no borrowings. You then need to compare this calculated yield to alternative investments.

An example

Let's look at an example to calculate the yields.

Tom	High risk investor	Tom will borrow £27,000 on an unsecured basis to raise the deposit of £25,000 and £2,000 acquisition costs. He will then obtain the other £75,000 by way of a mortgage to purchase the property.
Dick	Medium risk investor	Dick will fund the deposit and acquisition costs from his savings. He will then obtain the other £75,000 by way of a mortgage to purchase the property.
Harry	Low risk investor	Harry will fund the property price and acquisition costs with his savings.

Tom, Dick and Harry are all higher rate tax payers but they have very different risk profiles. They see a property advertised for £100,000 but all have very different strategies to buy the property.

They estimate that it can rent out for £1,000 per calendar month. They also estimate the following annual expenses to derive a profit and loss account.

	Tom	Dick	Harry
Rent	£12,000	£12,000	£12,000
Unsecured borrowing costs (interest only)	£1,750	N/A	N/A
Mortgage costs (interest only)	£4,500	£4,500	N/A
Void periods	£1,500	£1,500	£1,500
Service charges and ground rent	£1,000	£1,000	£1,000
Repairs	£500	£500	£500
Agents' fees	£1,050	£1,050	£1,050
Sundry	£450	£450	£450
Profit	**£1,250**	**£3,000**	**£7,500**
Tax @ 40%	£500	£1,200	£3,000
Net profit	**£750**	**£1,800**	**£4,500**

So the yields for each investor are as follows.

Investor	Calculation	Result
Tom – High risk investor	$$\frac{\text{(Annual rent – Annual mortgage cost – Annual loan cost – Expenses – Tax)} \times 100}{\text{(Deposit + Acquisition costs)}}$$ $$\frac{£750 \times 100}{£27,000}$$	2.8%
Dick – Medium risk investor	$$\frac{\text{(Annual rent – Annual mortgage cost – Expenses – Tax)} \times 100}{\text{(Deposit + Acquisition costs)}}$$ $$\frac{£1,800 \times 100}{£27,000}$$	6.7%
Harry – Low risk investor	$$\frac{\text{(Annual rent – Expenses – Tax)} \times 100}{\text{(Property purchase price + Acquisition costs)}}$$ $$\frac{£4,500 \times 100}{£102,000}$$	4.4%

Now all these yields are positive so the property purchase is expected to put money in the investor's pocket. What each of Tom, Dick and Harry's thresholds for investment are will determine whether they will buy. So for example if Tom's threshold is 4% to buy then he will not do so as the investment is below his 4% threshold. If Harry's threshold is 4% then Harry will buy as his yield is above his threshold. All of their thresholds will be based on their own personal criteria and alternative investments. But you can be assured that if the yields were negative then the professional investor would not be interested. This is because the investment will take money out of his pocket.

Understanding +/- yield

It's obvious to see that when the clock strikes 12 noon you are winning on both counts. That is to say that:

■ the yield is positive and at its highest point;
■ the capital growth is positive and at its highest point.

Looking at 12 noon graphically:

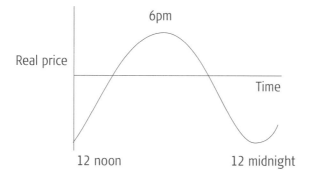

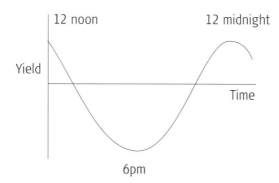

So we can see that at 12 noon the price of the property is at its lowest real price. As a result of this the yield is at its highest. Now due to the fact that rental prices are directly proportional to wages, which rise religiously with inflation, we can show that it's the property price alone that drives the yield. In other words the yield is only high due to the property purchase price being artificially low due to market conditions.

You have to draw on your own experiences to really believe what I'm saying. Just because house prices have risen by 20% in a year – do you ever see rental prices rising accordingly? Probably not. Rental prices are directionally proportional to wages. This makes sense. If you had volatile rental prices you would find that people would be on the streets! If interest rates rose dramatically, landlords would raise their rents to meet their mortgage payments and then 'forget' to reduce them as their mortgage payments fell. So as we have eliminated inflationary influences from this model we would have the rent vs time graph looking like this.

So we can see that rents do not change over time. Another great thing about rents are that they are:

■ known and
■ predictable.

They are known as it is very easy to gather the market rental value for a one, two or three bed property as there should be plenty of these types of properties to rent on the market. As long as the property you are thinking of buying is not unique in any way then the market rental value will be easily comparable with similar properties on the market. The rental market will not entertain a property that is over-priced on rent as the tenant will simply go elsewhere. So the market rent of a property will fall within a small range.

Rents are predictable as rental values only ever increase with wage inflation. So we can assume that the rents will rise but only modestly. Since we are ignoring inflation we can predict that rents will remain the same in real terms.

So using the graphs above we can see that over the four key points on the clock the yield is the inverse to the property purchase price, in other words, as property prices increase yields decrease:

	12 noon	3pm	6pm	9pm
Property price	£50,000	£116,667	£233,333	£116,667
Annual rent	£10,000	£10,000	£10,000	£10,000
Annual mortgage cost @ 6% interest of property price	£3,000	£7,000	£14,000	£7,000
Other costs	£3,000	£3,000	£3,000	£3,000
Net yield	£7,000	£nil	(£7,000)	£nil

So we can see that it's property prices that drive yield. In other words:

The property price is everything!

So knowing that the property price is everything we theoretically can ignore the yield curve as it is simply a result of the property price curve. An analysis of the property prices is essential if we want to gain heavily – so read on!

CHAPTER FOUR

Property Prices – Actual Prices, Real Prices and Bubbles

Let's look at the property price curve again:

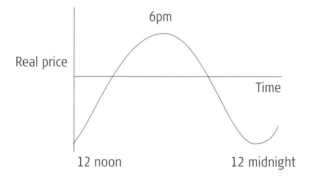

So at 12 noon we can see that the property price is at the lowest point below the real price. Now in order to find out if you have found an area that is in the 12 noon to 3pm range you need to compare the real price with the actual price the property can be bought for. So the two key figures in all of this are:

■ the actual price
■ the real price.

If the actual price is less than the real price then BINGO!

The actual price

We determine this as being 95% of the advertised price of a property. As an average properties sell at 95% of their asking price. So for example if we see a property advertised for £60,000 then the actual price will be:

$$£60,000 \times 95\% = £57,000$$

In reality the actual price is the price you can get the property for. It could be 95%, 100% or even 105% of the asking price dependent on how competitive the market is. However, under normal conditions 95% is about average.

The real price

Fundamental principles need to be applied when calculating the real price. The fundamental principles that apply to the property price are:

The greater of:

1. The price an investor is willing to pay
2. The price a first-time buyer is willing to pay

So whichever is greater out of these two figures will be the real price of the property. Therefore we need to calculate both of these prices.

The price a professional investor is willing to pay

A professional property investor would look for a return greater than a long term risk free rate. A good indicator of a long term risk free rate is the rate offered by the government on a **20 year fixed interest government gilt.**

A government gilt is a loan to the government. You can assume that the government will not go bankrupt so we can assume that it is risk free. Property is considered to be one of the next lowest risk investments out there. I reckon the professional property investor requires a minimum of a 2% loading on a 20 year fixed government gilt in order for them to invest.

This will determine the yield required and hence set the real value of the property. Lets look at an example:

Variables:

20 Year Fixed Interest Government Gilt	5.62%
Property Investor Loading	2.00%
Annual Rental Value of Property	£5,000

The real value would be:

$$\frac{£5,000 \times 1}{(5.62\% + 2.00\%)} = £65,616$$

This would be the maximum a professional investor would pay. This gives the property with a rental value of £5,000 per year a 7.62% yield. If the property price was higher then the professional property investor will seek an alternative investement such as another property in a different area or simply wait for a property to come within his price range.

The price a first-time buyer is willing to pay
The price a first-time buyer is willing to pay will be what banks are willing to lend. You would calculate this as follows:

$$\frac{\text{Their salary} \times 4}{(0.95)}$$

This assumes that lenders will lend four times the first-time buyer's salary if they put down a 5% deposit on the property. So, in the same example above, if a first-time buyer wants the same property and their salary is £21,000 then they could afford a purchase price of:

$$\frac{£21,000 \times 4}{0.95} = £88,421$$

So in this example the first-time buyer would outbid the professional investor and effectively 'win'. Thus the real value of the property would be set as £88,421.

So looking at the actual price compared to the real price we have:

Actual price	£57,000
Real price	£88,421
Under-valuation	**£31,421**

Looking at it split between the investor and the owner-occupier:

	Owner-occupier	Professional investor
Actual price	£57,000	£57,000
Real price	£88,421	£65,616
Under-valuation	£31,421	£8,616

We can see clearly that we are within the 12 noon to 3pm quarter. Both the investor and the owner-occupier are interested because to the prices each is willing to pay are above the actual price. We can see that the owner-occupier has more to gain in buying than the investor so aggressive bidding will occur thus pushing the price up quickly and dramatically. Looking at it in relation to the property price graph:

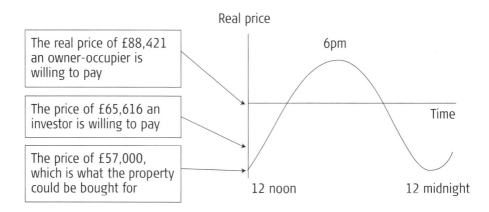

So we can see who drives property prices – we all do! It's our attitude that drives a property price not interest rates – even though all the city analysts believe that it does so. Interest rates do play a part but it's our propensity to borrow, the availability of borrowing, the willingness of lenders to lend and our fear of missing the boat that cause prices to rise.

What is happening between 3pm and 6pm? Effectively properties are being sold above the asking price. Using the same example as above let's say asking prices have rocketed to £100,000. Then we would have the actual price as:

$$95\% \times £100,000 = £95,000$$

Both the professional investor and owner-occupier prices will remain the same as nothing would have changed. That is to say that over the period of rocketing property prices the following would have remained stable:

- gilt rates
- salaries
- rental value of the property
- lending criteria of the banks.

So we would have the following table:

	Owner-occupier	Professional investor
Actual price	£95,000	£95,000
Real price	£88,421	£65,616
Over-valuation	**£6,579**	**£29,384**

This over-valuation is what I call the bubble element to the actual property price. Specifically the bubble element is £6,579 as it will be the lower of the two over-valuations. So in this case it is the owner-occupier because an owner-occupier has a higher valid bid price than the investor.

Looking at the graph again:

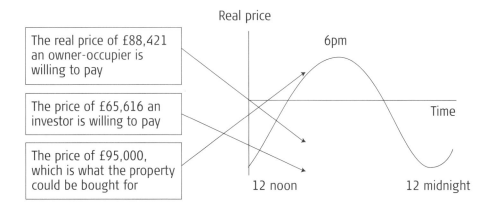

The real price of £88,421 an owner-occupier is willing to pay

The price of £65,616 an investor is willing to pay

The price of £95,000, which is what the property could be bought for

So who is buying at £95,000? Well it certainly isn't the:

- professional investor or
- standard owner-occupier.

The people who are buying at inflated prices are:

- **The speculative investor.** This investor is banking on prices rising at the same rate as in the past. Also if the stock market is under-performing then the attraction of the property market is heightened. They can buy and sell within a number of months or years and make a tidy profit. This type of investor can make money if they know when to sell but they will only be selling to another speculative investor or…

- **The scared owner-occupier.** This type of owner-occupier is scared of prices rising beyond affordability so they buy a property for more than it's worth, e.g. a professional working couple buying an unsuitable property to live in like a studio flat or an ex-local authority one-bed flat. They should wait for prices to fall so they can get a two-bed flat but their fear makes them buy a smaller property for an inflated price.

■ **The over-borrower.** This type of buyer will buy by using a deposit that has been raised by borrowing from a bank, credit card or loan company or get a self-certified mortgage where they lie about their income. Either one of these strategies results in over-borrowing. They also think, like the scared owner-occupier and speculative investor, that if they do not buy now they will miss out.

The best way to spot a bubble element is to calculate it. The equation holds, where 'P' = price:

$$\mathbf{P}actual = \mathbf{P}real + \mathbf{P}bubble$$
$\mathbf{P}$actual – The actual price of the property defined above
$\mathbf{P}$real – The real price of the property defined above
$\mathbf{P}$bubble – The difference between the actual price and the real price

So the bubble element exists when the actual price is greater than the real price. To spot bubble elements look at the following:

What to look for	Why
Type of property	If you're buying a studio flat for the price equivalent to five times the salary of the typical purchaser then a bubble element may exist as the property you are buying is unaffordable to the typical purchaser. It may not have a bubble element if the rental value stacks up – see below.
Type of purchaser	If you are considering buying a small one-bed flat that's in a city centre then consider what the average salary is for a worker in that city centre. Calculate what the average city worker could afford as they will be your main buyer as they invariably pay more than an investor. Can the city worker afford

What to look for	Why
	what you are paying? If they can't then you may be buying at an artificially high price unless it has a decent rental value – see below.
Rental value	What does the property yield? If the property yields greater than a 2% loading on the 20 year gilt rate then it's priced correctly. If it yields below then there may be a bubble element to the price.
Second and third time buyers	Bear in mind that people move up the property ladder and so there is a gain from the sale of their original property which contributes to the overall purchase price. If you are buying a two-bed home then it may be a second-time buyer that is the typical purchaser of this property. The real value will be four times their salary plus the estimated gain on their previous property. If you are paying more than they can afford then a bubble element may exist.
20 year government gilt figure	This is the long term investment risk free rate. There isn't much fluctuation in this figure but you could look at trends. Adding a 2% margin (or whatever you set) to this figure will determine the yield you require from any property investment.

What to look for	Why
Differential between long term rate and current rate	There are two types of interest rates: a long term fixed rate and a variable rate. So you could get a fixed rate for 10 years of 6% when the current variable rate is 5%. This would assume that rates are going to rise in the long term as the best rate you can get over the long term future is in excess of the current rate. If your model looks like it cannot cope with a higher rate in the future then you should consider selling or reducing your holding in the property market.
Rental value of property	The calculations above rely on an accurate figure for the annual rental amount receivable. Rents rise as well as fall so you should keep abreast of current rental values in order to calculate accurate real prices.
Current market value of property	If you're in the property game you have to keep track of property prices! This is the only way you're going to spot undervaluations. You need to see the price, determine the actual price, work out the real price, and then say to yourself "Oh – that's cheap, I'm going to buy!"

So in the last four chapters we have set out the basis for the property clock. Now let's get in to the detail of each quarter.

CHAPTER FIVE

12 noon to 3pm – Hot Spot

At the start – 12 noon

The clock strikes 12 noon – but there's no gong! At 12 noon hardly anyone knows that this area is a gold mine. It's a buyers' market. No one wants these properties and there are plenty of vendors desperate to sell. You walk in to the estate agents saying you want to buy and they roll out the red carpet! These agents have become accustomed to only vendors walking in to their office wishing to sell but at last they have stumbled across a buyer! You, with your hard earned cash and the bank's money, want to buy big time.

So you ask the agent what he has got. He then proceeds to pull out of his filing cabinet details of over 20 properties all yielding in excess of 12%! You ask him what the areas are like and he says they're fine. You're not so sure. You are always told never to believe an estate agent. You flick further through the details and you're seeing studios and one-bed flats yielding in excess of 20%. You ask to view all of the properties and to your surprise he says no problem. He then books half the day to show you all the properties. A lot of them are empty as no one wants them as investments and some of the areas look a bit rough. However, you can be assured that it is only a matter of time before other investors follow and regenerate the area to a solid rental area.

Now you have to be a brave man to buy when it's 12 noon. However, if you are brave, you will make the fortunes I have done as you have understood the concept of supply and demand. I had an email from someone who asked my advice. He was concerned that there was an oversupply of housing in Hull, East Yorkshire, and that if he bought a property it would not let out. I asked him 'well, what would it be like if it was the other way round – there was an under-supply of housing?' He would not have been sending me the email as the property prices in Hull would be much higher and thus not worth considering. So you have to go where there is low demand for property and wait for the demand to rise. And you can be sure it will rise as the only way is up.

12 noon – 3pm

Yields of 12% – 20% are unsustainable. If you were to find such a place that remained at this level you would be silly not to plough all of your savings and future income in to this area. This is because you will make a solid £50,000 out of every £100,000 invested if you geared up and bought wisely. If you took a risk you could make far more. However, a good thing never lasts forever. I will show you how it goes from 12 noon to 3pm. That is to say that the area goes from +growth and +yield to +growth and –yield.

Let's just say that it is not only me that has found this magic area that is yielding in excess of 12%. So I buy as much as I can afford from every estate agent in the area. As soon as something comes on the market that meets my criteria I buy without hesitation. It won't be long before another professional investor finds this area too as there a number of professional investors looking for these exact areas! Some professional investors have a high buying quota, sometimes in to the hundreds. I have a high quota, typically around 50, but there are much bigger sharks out there. So when other professional investors get wind of this magic area a bidding war commences.

It starts with properties being sold within 24 hours of the property coming on to the market at full asking price. This sends signals to the vendors that they are selling their properties too cheap so they increase their selling prices. Usually the vendors underestimate how much to put up their prices by (due to the market being stagnant only several months before and vendors simply can't believe that prices can get any higher) and professional investors pay over their asking price. This is because a professional investor has set criteria to buy to. For example I have a criteria of buying at 12% yield. So if I see a property for £30,000 and I know it will still yield 12% at £35,000, and it's a competitive market, then I would be silly not to offer £35,000 so as to ensure that I got the property.

What we then see is a rapid increase in prices. It's all about who will accept the lowest yield. The market quickly changes from a buyers' market to a sellers' market. All the time this is happening the owner-occupiers – typically first-time buyers – are trying to get a look in. They are even struggling to get properties as the investors are snapping them up before they've had a chance to even look at them.

Now, there are professional investors and owner-occupiers bidding in this market. Prices have risen dramatically. The speculative investor now gets wind of what has been going on. He has heard the stories of dramatic price increases and properties selling for over their asking price. The speculative investor is now thinking that they can buy a property, hold for a year or two and then sell at a massive profit. Let's welcome the speculative investor as a new entrant to the market.

The speculative investor is not the most clever of investors. It's unlikely that they do this as a full time profession but as a secondary source of income to their full time job. They may never have bought a property before apart from the one they live in (is this you?). This is where the errors start to occur. The speculative investor is not familiar with net yield and overestimates what the property will return. They overestimate the rent, underestimate the void periods, mortgage payments and repairs. However, blinded by the historic growth the speculative investor will push prices beyond the reach of the professional investor (as the professional investor now knows at that price it is a negative yield i.e. the property will take money out of his pocket) and out-bid the professional. Say goodbye to the good times because now at this point – the clock strikes 3pm.

Looking at this as a sweeping hand of the clock:

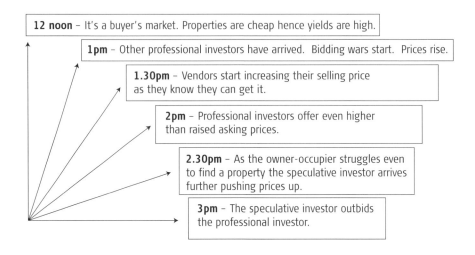

12 noon – It's a buyer's market. Properties are cheap hence yields are high.

1pm – Other professional investors have arrived. Bidding wars start. Prices rise.

1.30pm – Vendors start increasing their selling price as they know they can get it.

2pm – Professional investors offer even higher than raised asking prices.

2.30pm – As the owner-occupier struggles even to find a property the speculative investor arrives further pushing prices up.

3pm – The speculative investor outbids the professional investor.

Strategies within a hot spot

In a nutshell:

Borrow from everywhere and buy everything!

This may seem a bit extreme. But this is the only way you win at this game. You've got to bite the bullet and go for it. Hot spots do not last for long. I've seen hot spots go to cooling spots in three months. I've made £200,000 in capital growth for literally ten days' work of finding the right properties. And the funny thing is that this £200,000 will be accessed to buy in another hot spot and I'll simply repeat the process. This is how I have made a consistent £500,000 per year. So if you lock in your position in a hot spot early then you can sit back and watch your investments rocket as late entrants to the market bid prices up. The more you buy the more you make. It's as simple as that. This strategy has really only two real components:

■ Borrow from everywhere.
■ Buy everything.

Borrow from everywhere

You need to raise cash fast if you are going to exploit as much as you can within the hot spot. This cash will be used as deposits for each flat or house you choose to buy. Here are some quick ways of raising cash, starting with the cheapest first, to pump into a newly discovered hot spot.

Source	Cost	Narrative
Personal assets	0%	Sell all your *obsolete* assets. Notice I say obsolete assets. I am not saying sell the clothes off your back, just the assets you no longer use. This could be second cars, jewellery, paintings, or anything you have that could be of value. Do not worry if you have a certain attachment to something. You'll be able to buy it back with all the profits you make from following the property clock!
Savings	BoE base rate	If you've got savings then use them! The return you will be currently receiving will be well in to single digits so it really is a no brainer. Would you rather have a 35% return on your money or 5%?
Endowment policies or company shares	BoE base rate + 3%	If you have an IFA then speak to them before you do what I suggest as I shouldn't want you to seek me out for advising you in the wrong way. But my advice is: CASH THEM IN!

Source	Cost	Narrative
		You will never get rich by investing a few thousand pounds in well quoted stocks, shares or saving schemes. Whereas you at least stand a chance of making a lot of money from very little in property investment.
Borrow from family	BoE + 4%	You would be surprised how willing some of your older family members may be to lend you a bit of cash. They might be impressed that you want to do something about your retirement and are not doing the same as everyone else and doing NOTHING!
		A family member may be more willing to give you assets if you are proposing to invest it further, rather than simply squandering it on a new car or holiday.
		Some family members may see it as giving you your inheritance early. There are also some tax advantages for those worth more than £285,000 in giving you your inheritance early. Speak to your local accountant, but the basic rule of thumb is if they give you assets and they do not die within seven years then you get the assets free of inheritance tax.

Source	Cost	Narrative
Secured borrowings	BoE+2-7%	Secured borrowings means taking out loans with you offering the security of your assets, usually your own home. The cheapest way to do this is to go to your current mortgage lender and ask them for a further advance. Usually you can have the money within 14 days. If they say no then remortgage with another lender. There are so many products out there I'm sure you'll be able to find a deal that is better than your current mortgage. If that doesn't work then consider getting a second charge loan, which is where another lender lends on your existing equity in your home. These a bit more pricey but not that much when considering you will be investing in assets that will return you over 35% a year.
Unsecured borrowings	BoE+2-15%	**Loans** I've got many a loan from unsecured lenders. They charge anywhere from 6% right up to 30%, but are well worth it if you can find the right property investments. Approach your high street bank first, then the other high street banks, and then after that go to a broker. You can get a loan broker from reading the small ads in the national newspapers.

Source	Cost	Narrative
		Overdrafts Approach your current bank where you have your current account and ask them for an overdraft. I did this many years ago and to my surprise got £10,000. Last year I asked for a £100,000 overdraft. The decision didn't go my way but at least I asked ... **Credit cards** This is a great source of cheap finance. Yes, I did say cheap. One of my credit cards begs me to borrow for seven months at 0%. So I buy properties with this money, do the property up and then remortgage them. All due to the nice people at MBNA – thanks guys!
Get a partner	Dependent	This is the most expensive way to raise finance as they get a share. But its also the cheapest way to raise finance if the project goes bust! That's because the partner takes on the financial risk. If it's the only way you can enter the property market then do so, otherwise leave this strategy till last.

This is not an exhaustive list. You may have other good ideas for raising finance but if you can't raise the finance then you can forget the 'get rich quick' dream. It's as simple as that. You need money to make money. The great thing about property investment is that you do not need that much to participate. This is because the majority of the purchase price is funded by the bank (typically 85%). So if you want to buy £100,000 worth of property you need £15,000. If property prices double in a year (which happens sometimes in hot spots) then your £15,000 makes you £100,000. That's not bad for doing nothing!

Buy everything

Don't hang about, in other words. Check how much cash you've got and what you can get your hands on to work out how many properties you can buy. Once you have a set quota then see everything that's on the market. The way you get to see everything so that you get the best of what's available is as follows.

Action	Why
Get on every estate agent's mailing list	Find out all the contact details for every estate agent in the area. You can get this by visiting www.yell.com. Ring them up and tell them you are looking for properties up to £xxx,000, any type and any area. This will ensure that you will get a constant flow of opportunities in your letter box every other day.
Ring every estate agent	Properties come on to the market before the details have been printed. The only way you are going to find out about these properties is if you ring up and ask if anything new has come on since you last received their mailshot.
Visit every estate agent's website and set up email alerts	One way of getting details before they go to print is to go on the agent's website. If the agency is run well the site will be updated regularly and if you sign up with their email alert system you will instantly get the details of the new property as it is added. Some agents even have mobile sms text alerts!
Stay up there for a week	You may be competing with locals in the area. The only way you can compete with them is to be a local too! Find a cheap B and B, take a week off work and get hunting. A week's work in a hot spot can earn you four times your annual salary – and more!
Pay someone to look on your behalf	If you do work full time and you have a high buying quota then pay someone (you can trust!) to look on your behalf. Get them to take digital photos and get them to email them to you. I do this and pay them £10 per property. If he finds one property worth buying out of 25 then he's done well. He actually

Action	Why
	finds one property out of every two that's worth buying so he does fantastically.
Check local press	Some deals I have found have been in the local paper. Some people hate estate agents and refuse to pay their high selling fees. Why pay over £1,000 to a slick agent when you can pay your local paper £10 for a small box ad? Scan all local press for property ads.

CHAPTER SIX

3pm to 6pm – Cooling Spot

Cooling starts – 3pm

Picking up from the last chapter – the speculator has out-bid the professional. So all that remain are the speculative investors and the owner-occupiers. These types of purchasers have very different agendas. The speculative investor is looking to make money and the owner-occupier is looking for somewhere to live. Bearing in mind that the speculative investor is essentially a novice, their buying choices will largely be drawn on their own experiences with property. This will be likely limited to purchases that they have made for themselves to live in. In effect the speculative investor has the same buying requirements as the owner-occupier as they are the same being but with different agendas! The speculative investor will buy on emotion rather than fundamentals just the same as the owner-occupier. So they will be lured into the same property developer traps as the normal owner-occupier falls into. Common errors made by speculative investors are:

■ A higher purchase price will be paid by a speculative investor for a property that conforms to their higher décor standards, disregarding the prospective tenant's lower décor standards. The standard of décor that is required for rental properties will be over-estimated with the belief that the tenant will pay for this higher standard and that the tenant will maintain it.

■ A bias towards private up-market areas as the speculative investor feels 'safe' in these areas. A speculative investor will be typically earning above the average UK salary and will expect their tenants to be 'young professionals'. What they fail to understand is that the young professional sector are either looking to buy themselves, and may very well be a competitor for the type of properties the speculative investor is looking at, or they will have assistance from parents in the buying process. Soon private developments become a fierce bidding ground with only one winner – the property developer!

■ Properties that require refurbishment look like the only type of properties that the owner-occupier can afford due to their 'perceived' undesirability. Unfortunately only the opposite is true! Speculative investors look at the past historical growth and consider these type of properties another goldmine. They assume that after refurbishment they can make a nice tidy profit and have the opportunity to display their interior design skills for all to see. Again the speculative investor overestimates the sale price and underestimates the repair work and bids higher than the owner-occupier.

■ Assuming that a tenant will be grateful and less fussy when deciding on whether to rent a property. Box rooms will be tolerated by the owner-occupiers but not by a tenant who may have to sleep in this box room! There is an arrogance element to the speculative investor assuming the tenant will be grateful for the high finish of the property even though the property is under-sized.

So as these two types of purchaser walk into the estate agents the red carpet is definitely not rolled out! The estate agent would have seen at least 20 of you already and to be honest is fed up with them saying either 'I'm looking for a property to buy to rent out' or 'I'm looking for a property to get me on the property ladder' – change the record! You, as a professional investor, look around at their display of properties on the wall, you see a property that looks cheap, but damn, it says 'under offer'. You look further around and you see that all the properties on the wall are under offer or sold. You ask the estate agent what she's got under £100k and she hands you one sheet. It's a studio flat, requiring upgrading and it's on a lease of less than 50 years! Any property that looks mildly interesting is above £150k and yielding less than 6.5%. You leave, leaving the speculative investor and the owner-occupier to battle it out.

3pm - 6pm

So what causes an owner-occupier to outbid a speculative investor? An owner-occupier will buy a property based on what they can afford, a speculative investor will pay whatever covers their estimated expenses. Whoever is higher will win. Look at this example:

Advertised property price	£100,000
Rental value p.a.	£7,000

The speculative investor

If the rental value is £7,000 then their mortgage company will allow them £7,000/130% = £5,384. This is because any buy to let mortgage company will lend only if the rent is 130% or greater than the mortgage payments. The investor can now use the rent to pay the mortgage and benefit from the expected capital growth that they estimate at no cost to themselves – essentially money for nothing! So at current borrowing rates of 5% the amount the speculative investor can go to is:

$$\frac{\text{Maximum annual mortgage payment}}{\text{current borrowing rate}}$$

$$\frac{£5,384}{5\%} = £107,680$$

The owner-occupier

The typical purchaser for this type of property, looking to live in it, is earning £20,000. Their buying power will be their level of deposit and the mortgage they can raise. Based on a £10,000 deposit and four times lending the owner-occupier could stretch to:

$$£10,000 + (4 \times £20,000) = £90,000$$

So we can see that the speculative investor wins and thus will outbid the owner-occupier and push the price beyond £90,000 into the hands of the speculator. So the speculator will get the property between £90,000 and £100,000. Then you are left with just the speculator battling it out with other speculators and thus pushing the price to £107,680. What the speculative investor has not factored in is:

- void periods
- tenant default
- interest rate rises
- repairs
- exit strategy.

The only thing that can push the price beyond the £107,680 mark is other owner-occupiers increasing their buying power by teaming up or by the individual seeking high income-multiple lenders. So in this example if you had two owner-occupiers deciding to live together and buy, both on the same salary and deposit, then their combined buying power would be:

$$£10,000 + £10,000 + (2.75 \times £40,000) = £130,000$$

This assumes a 2.75 times joint salary which is standard within the mortgage market.

So now the property's value has risen to what a couple would be willing to pay for it. This couple could quite comfortably afford it even with expected interest rate rises as this is the home that they have chosen and their borrowing has been underwritten to be no more than 2.75 times joint salary.

So we can see there is a point when even the speculative investor drops out and is outbid by the owner-occupier accepting a lower standard property. Even speculative investors who are holding now sell out to owner-occupiers as the speculative investors are losing money on a monthly basis (due to rents not covering the mortgage and other expenses) even though they are gaining on capital growth.

If it had been an individual seeking a high income-multiple lender then their buying power could have been:

£10,000 + (4.93 x £20,000) = £108,600

4.93 times individual salary being the highest income multiple I could find in the mortgage market as of today. This still outbids the speculative investor.

Looking at it as a sweeping hand of the clock:

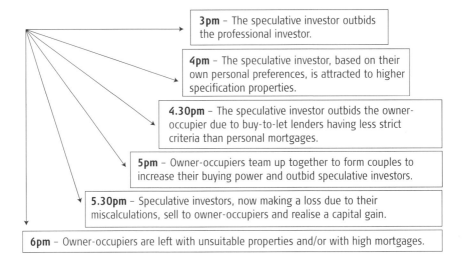

3pm – The speculative investor outbids the professional investor.

4pm – The speculative investor, based on their own personal preferences, is attracted to higher specification properties.

4.30pm – The speculative investor outbids the owner-occupier due to buy-to-let lenders having less strict criteria than personal mortgages.

5pm – Owner-occupiers team up together to form couples to increase their buying power and outbid speculative investors.

5.30pm – Speculative investors, now making a loss due to their miscalculations, sell to owner-occupiers and realise a capital gain.

6pm – Owner-occupiers are left with unsuitable properties and/or with high mortgages.

Strategies within a cooling spot

The professional investor has dropped out of the market at this point. So if you consider yourself as a professional then the strategy is not to buy. If you want to make money in a cooling spot then you have no option but to buy and then sell. In other words you have to property trade. Now I am no expert on property trading and there is a good reason for this – I've never done it! It's a risky game to play. I believe in the old mantra that property is a 'long term investment'. A lot of money can be made but also can be lost. If you get your figures wrong and the market turns then you can get really stung.

However, considering it is the only strategy we have within a cooling spot, we'd best look at it in further detail. To make a profit from buying a property then subsequently selling it, the property has to experience capital appreciation. Capital appreciation can be amassed by one of two ways:

■ Identifying properties with foresight.
■ Identifying properties with potential.

1. Identifying properties with foresight

This is what people think they're good at – speculating. You need to be extremely clever to do this as it requires an analysis of all the variables in the property market and make a prediction based on what is already out in the public domain.

The typical properties that perform well in a rising market are:

■ Unique properties that are scarce such as detached houses in London, four bed properties where there's a glut of three bed properties, or riverside properties.

■ The more exclusive end of the market such as gated developments, prestigious addresses and better located properties in prime locations.

■ Properties in a well serviced area with good schools, train stations, leisure facilities and shopping malls.

■ New build properties.

■ Areas under regeneration.

The estimated returns from the above type of investments is difficult to gauge. This is because:

1. You do not have all the information to hand to be able to analyse and quantify the extra growth likely to be experienced based on all these desirable extras.

2. You are asking private individuals what they think these extras are worth. If the property is sufficiently unique then this could be absolutely any figure! Try thinking along the lines of what would Michael Jackson pay for a house in London with a fully equipped theme park in the back garden????

To try and quantify these extras you need to take in to account the qualitative factors and try to put a value to these.

Take for example a five bed detached home in Camden in London. How many properties like this are there for sale in Camden – lets say eight? Out of those, how many people want or need to sell? Let me tell you – very few! How many people are actively looking for a house with a garden in Camden? Abolutely loads! So for rare and highly desired properties it's a seller's market.

Now if you can sit on your money you can literally drive prices up. It's up to you when you sell and for how much unless you are forced to sell for reasons out of your control. Its called 'Name your price!' You name the price and they have to pay it – and usually they do. This is why the property prices at the exclusive end of the London market, and prestigious homes located in the home counties but commutable to London, have gone through the roof. Rises of up to 50% in one year have been seen for homes in London at the £5m mark. That means some people have bought a property for £5m and then had it valued at £10m! Nice work when you can get it.

If you want to speculate on what to speculate on then look at commute times. It seems that leisure time is getting more and more important and saving five minutes on a commute is deemed to be very attractive. If you can find something that little bit closer to the city then you could get an above average gain over the next coming years compared to a property outside of the city.

2. Identifying properties with potential

Now if you want to make money the hard way and do something to a property then you can always get your DIY tool box out. I try to stay away from this but that's because I am lazy! However there are people who make a living out of this and have even got a TV series out of it, like Sarah Beeney, so I have to include it in this book!

With a residential property you can either:

a) Refurbish it.
b) Extend the property.
c) Convert the loft.

a) Refurbish it

There is real synergy to be created if you get this right. Synergy means the sum is greater than the parts, or some people like to say 2+2 = 5. Let me explain.

John buys a house for £200,000. Spends £10,000 refurbishing it and sells immediately for £250,000. So he makes £250,000 – (£200,000 +£10,000) = £40,000. So in this example:

$$£200k + £10k = £250k$$

£40k has appeared like magic from seemingly nowhere. The reason for this £40k appearing is due to:

■ **John saving time for the buyer.** Part of this £40,000 represents time and hassle taken out of the buyer's equation. If the buyer saw the property for £200,000 it would not be attractive as they could neither do the work nor project manage it.

■ **John having £10,000 to refurbish it in the first place.** Having the money to refurbish a property cuts most buyers out. The usual people who have an extra £10,000 in the bank on top of the deposit to buy the property are property investors like me, not private individuals. This makes the property more difficult to buy and hence these investors bid the price down.

■ **John is an expert.** The cost to refurbish a property for a developer is VERY different to the cost achievable by a private individual. This is because developers know where to shop, what not to do and how to make things look better than what they cost. This is because it is their livelihood and they need to know these tricks and tips. These all result in making the property appear more valuable than what they have put in. Its called 'adding value'.

I said above I don't really get involved in refurbishments, however this is not strictly true. I do but only when I am forced to. This is when either the property

a) is so cheap that I can't say no
b) the property gets vandalised by the tenant or kids on the street
c) and when I do, I do the bare minimum.

Now there are loads of books on how to add value to a property by making it look pretty and this ain't one of them! The market is flooded with amateur DIYers who have given up their day jobs to pursue this activity. What is actually happening is that properties requiring work actually go for more than properties that don't require any work at all! If you are going to enter this market ensure you do not underestimate your costs and overestimate your selling price. Have a look at this example:

There's a property for sale for £100,000 that would be worth £150,000 if it was refurbished under current market conditions. The cost of the refurbishment is estimated at £10,000 and will take two months. I would adopt this forecasted profit and loss:

Selling price (90% of anticipated selling price) = 90% x £150,000	£135,000
Estate agents' fees 1% +VAT	(£1,586)
Net proceeds	£133,413
Costs:	
Purchase price	£100,000
Refurbishment (150% x estimated costs)	£15,000
Loan repayments (six months' interest)	£2,500
Total costs	(£117,500)

Anticipated profit   **£15,913**

So prudently it will take you six months to make £15,913. Annualised its £31,826. Now is this worth your time? If you left a £10,000 p.a. job then maybe this project would have been worthwhile. If you left a £70,000 p.a job then maybe not.

b) Extend the property

Extending a property is a guaranteed way to increase its value. However, this is not a guarantee that you will add any value. You could actually spend £10,000 and only add value of only £8,000. I have created a way of avoiding such a hiccup.

It's all to do with the ratio of land to buildings cost. If you build on prime land then you win, if not you lose!

So what is prime land? Well it's all to do with the rebuild cost of the property. You can get this from the original survey you had carried out when you bought it originally. If the survey was carried out a while ago then allow for price inflation of around 2.5% for each year on the rebuild cost.

To decide if the land is prime you simply calculate the following ratio:

$$\frac{\text{Current market value}}{\text{Rebuild cost}}$$

If the ratio is greater than 1 then it's prime. If its less than 1 then it's not prime.

So if Jack has a property that is currently worth £100,000 and the rebuild cost is £60,000 then the current market value rebuild ratio is:

$$\frac{£100,000}{£60,000} = 1.667$$

which is greater than 1, hence Jack should extend.

If Jill also has a property worth £100,000 and it has a rebuild cost of £120,000 then the ratio is:

$$\frac{£100,000}{£120,000} = 0.833$$

which is less than 1, hence Jill should not extend.

You should use this ratio as a multiplier to determine how much value will be added to the property. So in the above examples if they both decided to spend £30,000 on a downstairs extension then their properties, as a rule of thumb, increase by:

1.667 x £30,000 = £50,000 for Jack
0.833 x £30,000 = £25,000 for Jill

So Jack makes £50,000 – £30,000 = £20,000 profit as a result of the extension, Jill makes £25,000 – £30,000 = £5,000 loss as a result of the extension.

This ratio is only an indication and should not be used as an exact estimating tool. This is because there is a lot more to an extension, such as choice of materials, style and design and so on. However, if the ratio is greater than 2 then it should be taken as a big green light to EXTEND! This is because whatever you spend you will approximately get twice back.

c) Convert the loft

This is the cheapest way to get an extra bedroom. For some reason in this country we determine the worth of a property largely on the number of bedrooms rather than the arbitrary measure of square footage. You must use this anomaly to your advantage. To calculate whether you should or should not convert the loft use the multiplier above but multiply it by 3. Let me show you using the same example above:

Jack's multiplier: 1.667 x 3 = 5.00
Jill's multiplier: 0.833 x 3 = 2.5

These are both Jack and Jill's loft multipliers. So if Jack and Jill both spend £5,000 on a loft conversion then they can expect an uplift in the values of their homes by:

Jack: 5.00 x £5,000 = £25,000
Jill: 2.5 x £5,000 = £12,500

So Jack and Jill can expect to profit from their loft conversion to the tune of £20,000 and £7,500 respectively.

The buyers in a cooling spot

There is no point in selling when your property is currently in a hotspot. This is because there is still room for the price to grow and it's currently profitable thus its not costing you to hold. It becomes worth selling only when the property becomes unprofitable but the price is still growing. **The highest point in the market can only ever exist within a Cooling Spot.** This is because the property price has risen to the point that it is unprofitable but it is still on a trend upwards. A professional investor drops out of buying in this market and only the owner-occupiers and novice investors remain.

You will be able to sell within this market as it exists as there will be owner-occupiers who will not be concerned about the profitability of a property as they wish to live in it rather than rent it out. There are also speculative investors out there who are banking on the property price to keep on growing and the novice investor who doesn't do their sums right. These buyers are able to buy your property at an inflated price above the real price because:

Owner-occupier	
Self-certified borrowing	Self-certified borrowing means that you can self-certify your income. You do not need to prove your income. All you need to do is state your income. This has led to people lying about what they earn even though they can afford the mortgage. This means they bypass the restriction of income multiples of around 4 times genuine salary and get borrowings of 4 times *fictitious* salary. This pushes up the prices paid above the normal fundamental prices and creates a bubble.
High income multiple lending	Some lenders are offering in excess of 4 times salary. I have seen 6 times salary for certain types of working individuals, such as trainee doctors and solicitors. This can cause a bubble element to property prices as these types of borrowers can outbid the normal 4 times salary buyer. It then becomes a battle between these professional salaried workers with only one winner – the vendor!

| Consumer debt | Due to the banks seeming willing to lend to absolutely anyone for virtually anything, everyone seems to have a deposit. This has increased the number of buyers and hence pushed demand for property higher. Higher demand means higher prices which are achievable due to borrowing a bigger deposit which is usually not stress tested for affordability. |

Novice investor and speculative investor

| Buy to let | Due to the buy to let mortgage also operating under the current variable base rate the same problem occurs here. Instead of demanding a 2% loading over the long term rate they demand a 2% loading over the current variable base rate. This means you get novice investors buying at 6% yields and below, hence superceding the first time buyers highest price. |
| | Due to the poor performance of the stock market in recent years the property market has attracted the traditional stock market investor. Here the investor will aim for capital growth and so will be happy to take a less than 2% loading. The speculative investor will make the estimation that the growth experienced in the past will happen in the future over the short term. The speculative investor's bid then supercedes the first-time buyer's bid hence a bubble element will exist. |

It is these types of buyers that do cause the bubble in the property market – so use them to your advantage! To find out about where all the hotspots, cooling spots, coldspots and warmspots are in the UK then visit www.propertyhotspots.net. (This site also has a national yield and capital growth index for over 330 areas in the UK.)

Awareness table	
Ratio of earnings to property value	The industry standard is around 4 to 4.25. So keep track of average salaries in an area and their size relative to property prices in that area. Look at typical first-time buyer properties and typical first-time buyer salaries in differing industries.
Lending multiples	Its around 4 to 4.25 as said earlier but it used to be 3! So it has crept up over time which therefore changes the fundamental price of a property.
Number of first-time buyers	The market starts with first-time buyers. If there is a lack of these then prices have to fall as they are not taking the bait. Investors will step in but only to a certain degree. The market requires first-time home owners in order to rise the property ladder, otherwise second-time property prices will fall dramatically.

CHAPTER SEVEN

6pm to 9pm – Cold Spot

6pm...it's getting cold

So now we have owner-occupiers buying properties that are too small for what they're worth, and owner-occupiers with high income multiple mortgages, but not a speculative or professional investor in sight. The market has gone stagnant. Renters are unwilling to buy and move into a property that is smaller than what they are renting, owner-occupiers are stuck into a property that is not growing as before, speculative investors are not interested because on the face of it there is no gain to be had and the professional investor has long gone due to it being unprofitable at 3pm. So who is left buying? The owner-occupier! The owner-occupier is overstretching themselves by accepting unsuitable properties or going to high income multiple lenders (the self-certified borrower who has lied about their income is also buying but this is a small percentage of the overall buyers at 6pm).

The inevitable is about to happen. Interest rates will rise. This is the only thing that can jolt the market. Now I'm not saying a few quarter point interest rate rises. I'm talking about a 2%+ rise from its lowest point. This is when it begins to hurt.

Two terms then start to rear their ugly heads (in order):

1. Negative equity.
2. Repossession.

Negative equity
This, in simple terms, is when the mortgage balance is greater than the value of the house. This in itself is not a problem over the long-term as the value of the house will recover. It is a big problem for:

- **owner-occupiers** who wish to move;
- **lenders** wishing to access their security on defaulting borrowers;
- **the economy** due to the feel-good factor being lost, hence a reduction in spending;
- **the property market** as fewer property deals are done thus estate agents, brokers and other industries surrounding the property market feel the pinch.

Repossession

This is when the lender legally enforces the sale of a property they have lent on due to the borrower defaulting on their mortgage payments. This situation occurs when:

- **interest rates** rise making the mortgage repayments unaffordable;
- **job losses** happen within the household so the mortgage payments become unaffordable.

The number of repossessions occurring every month are directly related to the economy as repossessions are a function of interest rates and job losses. So if interest rates rose to 20% and / or everyone lost their job then everyone would get repossessed and lose their home. If interest rates were 0% and unemployment rates were 0% then no one would lose their home. We are somewhere in between.

6pm – 9pm

So at 6pm we only have the owner-occupiers buying unsuitable properties at inflated prices or obtaining finance from high income multiple lenders. Property prices now reach their maximum. This is due to married (or co-habiting) owner-occupiers being unable to buy as lending is restricted to 2.75 times joint salary or individual owner-occupiers being restricted to 4.93 times salary. Speculative investors are unable to buy as lending is restricted to 130% of the mortgage payment. The buyers at 6pm are the last weight of buyers and are buying at the peak. As usual the private individual is the one who suffers – they buy high and are forced to sell low. These buyers have not factored in interest rate rises. There are also owner-occupiers who have previously bought and accessed their equity from high income-multiple lenders (greater than four times salary) and second charge lenders with less strict lending criteria. They have ignored warnings that rates will rise.

Rates do begin to rise, but only modestly, to attract overseas investment in government gilts to fund the deficit being experienced as a result of over-consumption. The press start to hint at negative equity spreading across thousands of households in the future due to the now upward trend of interest rates. Repossession rates are followed closely by the press to see if they are increasing month by month. If there is an increase you can be sure it's front page news on some of the tabloids. A sense of fear sets in even though there has been no real change in property prices. Properties for sale remain in the windows of estate agents with none of the vendors willing to drop their prices (because they don't have to) and none of the buyers able to afford what is for sale.

TV ads for loans start to decline. Stories of how people have made a fortune in property now seem stale and also unrealistic within the current environment. Some speculative investors who were breaking even are now losing money due to the slight increase in interest rates. The speculative investor is not forced to sell (due to the loss being only small and manageable) but chooses to sell as the investment is taking money out of their pocket and they can bank a gain if they sell now. So several properties come onto the market requiring a quick sale from the speculative investors. As they already have a gain locked in the speculative investor will reduce their price for a genuine quick sale. Property prices start to reduce and creep back to affordable levels. Some speculators are lucky and sell to frustrated owner-occupiers dying to get on the property ladder. Other speculative investors are not so lucky as owner-occupiers get wise and think it's better to wait and see if prices drop further or if a better property comes on to the market…

Rates rise again. And again. Repossession rates have risen for the first time and it's splashed over the press. Certain areas are reported to be in negative equity. The owner-occupier seeking a home to buy is now smiling as they think property prices will drop further. Estate agents are convincing their vendors to reduce their prices to attract people through the door. Lenders are losing as a result of the repossessions as after all legal costs have been taken into account the monies raised from the sale do not cover the amount they lent and all other costs of repossession. Lenders start to restrict lending. This further stagnates the market. Property prices fall further.

Second charge lenders and unsecured lenders start experiencing defaults due to the borrower choosing to pay their mortgage rather than their second charge and unsecured debts. Regret for the holidays and cars that were bought with this money starts to set in. People start to restrict what they spend on the high street and try to liquidise some of the assets bought with their remortgaged money. Suddenly saving seems better than spending! The feel-good factor has now been lost. Property prices start falling further due to the lack of buyers.

Speculative investors are now happy to get back what they had paid for the property as it is better to get rid of a property that is costing them every month. The gain once promised from these properties fails to materialise. Some speculative investors actually lose capital to obtain a quick sale. Property investment starts to get a bad name. Some speculative investors see some of their hard-earned savings lost to free them from the bind of the poor performing investment property or properties.

Rates rise further. Repossession rates rise further. Everyone who had bought at 6pm is now in negative equity. More and more owner-occupiers are struggling to pay their mortgages and they want to sell. The market gets flooded with properties for sale by desperate vendors. The problem is it is neither a buyers' market nor a sellers' market! Some are lucky and sell to other owner-occupiers, others are not so fortunate and get repossessed. All the owner-occupiers who had overstretched themselves by over-borrowing can no longer meet the higher repayments produced by the interest rate rises. Supply of property is now well in excess of demand. Prices have to fall even further.

The only real saviour in this falling market, with any kind of buying clout to prevent prices falling to ridiculous levels, is the professional investor. At 9pm they see that prices have fallen to a level where, if they were to buy, the purchase will put money into their pocket at a rate greater than leaving the money in the bank even though property prices are falling. So, the clock strikes 9pm. Welcome back the professional investor.

Looking at it as a sweeping hand of the clock:

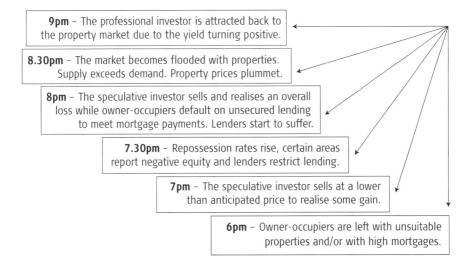

9pm – The professional investor is attracted back to the property market due to the yield turning positive.

8.30pm – The market becomes flooded with properties. Supply exceeds demand. Property prices plummet.

8pm – The speculative investor sells and realises an overall loss while owner-occupiers default on unsecured lending to meet mortgage payments. Lenders start to suffer.

7.30pm – Repossession rates rise, certain areas report negative equity and lenders restrict lending.

7pm – The speculative investor sells at a lower than anticipated price to realise some gain.

6pm – Owner-occupiers are left with unsuitable properties and/or with high mortgages.

Strategies within a cold spot

There is no money to be made here. Anything you buy will take away whatever you put in by way of a deposit and take money out of your pocket every month – ouch! If an area is a cold spot then simply avoid it. If you own a property in a cold spot and you can get out with a gain then do so. If you own a property in a cold spot and cannot get out with a gain then oh dear! You will be experiencing the following:

1. Having a property that is in negative equity.
2. Having a property that is costing you to hold every month.

Now you can sell but it will cost you capital to get out. I would not advise this as you are realising a capital loss. Property is a long-term investment and prices will recover so there is no point in realising a loss if you are able to. So the only strategy left to you is to fund the difference every month from your own pocket. This requires cash. Ways to raise cash to fund the monthly shortfall are to:

1. Liquidise assets you have now.
2. Save some of the income you earn now.
3. Increase your income.

1. Liquidise assets you have now

Here is a list of assets that you may have that have some value to someone. That is to say that you could sell, liquidise or cash in on these assets and raise cash, as there is a ready market for these types of assets. The best places to advertise these items are in the local press, internet or papers such as *loot* or *Ad-Trader*. If you can't be bothered then take the items to dealers in your area.

Asset	Justification
Cars	How important is the car you have for your day-to-day activities? Do you commute to work by public transport Monday to Friday, drink at the weekends and only use the car to ferry your weekly household shopping? Have you ever considered getting a taxi or shopping online? All the major supermarkets offer online shopping – some offer free delivery. If the car's not that important you can raise cash from the sale of the car plus save on the ongoing

running and maintenance costs. Running a car costs anywhere from £50 to £500. This can easily rise to above £1,000 if you take into account the HP payment if it's on HP. Selling a car can have a dramatic impact on cashflow as not only does it raise cash – it saves cash.

If the car is important to you then consider trading your car in for a cheaper alternative.

Jewellery

Do you have any jewellery that you no longer and never intend to wear? It is a waste to have these items. Look at these items as if they are cash. There are plenty of jewellery shops out there that have cash ready and waiting. Don't worry if all it raises is £150 – it's still £150! This all goes in to the kitty. Remember, you've got to start somewhere.

Furniture, collections and other household goods

Do you own an expensive record collection that you never touch? I know I do – but I don't need the money now! When I was younger though I used to DJ. I would sell my old records (and when I say old, I mean six months out of date) to raise cash to buy up-to-date records. This kept me getting booked for gigs.

Unused goods, collections, furniture or other items can just sit there and eventually end up in a boot sale, jumble sale or even worse – the rubbish bin. Do any of your goods that you no longer use have a value now? Not only can you raise cash but you can also de-clutter your living space.

Asset	Justification
Electrical equipment	TVs, videos, DVD players, hi-fis are easy ways to raise cash. Also the actual cassettes can raise you more than you think. There are many second-hand exchange type of stores, such as Cash Converters, that will pay you for these types of goods.
Obsolete items	Look around your house and garage. Is there anything that you don't use? Now does it have value? The best way to gauge if it has value is to ask yourself – how much did I pay for this thing? If it was substantial, say over £100, and you could imagine someone else using it, then it's probably worth something to somebody.

2. Saving some of the income you earn now

There are really only two core ways of saving money:

a) Going without i.e. not spending!
b) Cutting costs i.e. spending less!

a) Not spending. I'm not going to bore you about how you should stop smoking, drinking, eating or just simply indulging. What you should do is when you get paid pay out all your fixed costs first as these are non-negotiable. So the shortfall should be paid as soon as you get paid. What will happen is that you'll adjust to the new level of spending that you have at your disposal.

Always ask yourself – do I really need this item that I'm buying now or do I just want it? Is it a need or a want? If it's a luxury item then it's probably a want. When I was setting up my property business I went without. Here are some of the things that I used to buy when I was at work but went without when I was starting self-employment:

- newspapers and magazines
- use of a whole flat (I switched to shared accommodation)
- CDs
- designer clothes
- meals at restaurants
- nights out in London visiting trendy bars and nightclubs.

It was easy for me to go without. In the back of my mind I knew that what I went without now I would have in the future.

b) Spending less. There are really only five things you can spend your money on:

  i) food and consumables
 ii) shelter
iii) travel
 iv) entertainment and clothing
  v) loans and savings plans.

Here are some tips on how to cut back on spending on each of these categories.

i) Food and consumables
Eat in rather than out. It's so easy to go to down to your nearest burger chain, Indian restaurant or Chinese take-away. There's no washing up, it tastes lovely and there is no preparation time involved.

However, you do pay for this! I used to make myself sandwiches in the poor days. Two slices of bread, a bit of lettuce and a chicken slice – total cost 20p! Compare this to an Indian take-away costing £7 at least. Now I'm not saying don't treat yourself. I treated myself to one chicken biryani from my local Indian once a week – but that was it.

Invariably the food you will prepare at home will be healthier too. The irony is that even though I can afford to eat out every night I now choose to eat in as it is healthier. I even look forward to those chicken sandwiches now!

Go round to your Mum's! Now this may not be possible for everyone. It depends on whether she is still alive, you still see her or if you live close to her. The principle is – don't be ashamed to ask for help. My mum quite enjoyed seeing me twice a week (or sometimes more!) and likewise – there's no cooking like your mum's cooking.

Do you have a brother, sister, nan, cousin or good friend who loves to see you? If you let them know what you are doing – trying to preserve your property portfolio – then you will be surprised, they are more than willing to help.

Do not think you are a sponger! Always remember people who help you get to the top. As thanks my mum now receives an income from me that is in excess of her pension and she doesn't have to do a thing!

Try non-branded goods. If you understand how supermarkets work then you will try this. A lot of 'own brand' goods are produced by the branded goods manufacturers. Sometimes the quality is the same. Now I say sometimes! I have tried some of the non-branded goods and they taste awful but there are some own-branded goods that taste as good if not better than the branded goods. So give it a try. The savings can be up to 50%.

Buy one get one free. Every supermarket does this. They sell goods at no profit or even at a loss to get you through the door. You can use this to your advantage. If you have the time you can go to every major supermarket and capitalise on all of their deals. I have to admit, I never had the time to justify the cost savings. But if you have a family and you are willing to stock up then I would estimate that you can reduce your shopping bill by 40%.

ii) Shelter
Switch utilities suppliers. It's a competitive market out there when it comes to supplying gas, electricity and telephone. Due to deregulation you can save up to 40% on your bills simply by switching and it is an easy thing to do!

Look out for new tariffs for your mobile phone. Prices have only come down since their introduction and so there will always be a new tariff being introduced that will trump your existing tariff sooner or later.

Shop around for contents insurance. The insurance market is a competitive one. Do not accept the premiums you have to pay just because you paid it last year. Get in contact with a good insurance broker to get you the best deal.

Have you ever considered not getting insurance? Sometimes you can pay a hefty premium to insure not a lot – and even then you don't get a pay out when you make a claim!

iii) Travel

Sell the car. Owning and running a car is not cheap. You've got HPI payments, insurance premiums, road tax duty, petrol and oil costs, servicing costs and repairs. That's a lot of expenses! You could save a small fortune if you did sell the car.

Do a feasibility test on the car. Work out how much you spend a month on the car and see if it is greater than if you walked, cycled, took the train or bus and took taxis. If it is – then it's time to sell the car! Remember a car is a luxury item. Public transport is supposed to be getting better and providing better value for money so be brave – get rid of it!

Downsize the car. Okay, it may not be practical to get rid of the car but how about downsizing it?

- Consider a smaller car with a smaller engine – this will cut fuel costs.
- Consider a lower insurance grouped car. Even consider third party only insurance. When was the last time you had an accident? Statistically you are unlikely to have an accident that is your fault if you haven't had an accident in the last five years.
- Maybe sell the car on HPI and buy a cheap run-around thus saving on the loan repayments.

- Road tax is reduced by £60 per year if you drive a car with less than a 1.5 litre engine.
- Get the car serviced by a non-main dealer.

Try walking or get a bike! If you don't have a car but get buses, trains and/or taxis then consider walking or cycling. You will save on the fares and it will keep you fit!

iv) Entertainment and clothing

Shop in the sales, markets and charity shops. One of my good friend's dad told me that he buys his winter suits in summer and his summer suits in winter. The key is to get value for money. If you're shopping in a glitzy, air conditioned, fashionable part of town then you are paying for it! All the expensive rents, rates and décor they have to pay for are ultimately paid by you because they charge you a high mark up on the goods sold.

You'll be surprised how well stocked some of the market traders are now. I still get most of my designer clothes from markets and superstores – not New Bond Street in London W1!

Think about if it's a need or a want. As mentioned above you need to always ask yourself if it's a need or a want. Do you really need to see the latest releases at the cinema or can you wait a year when they hit the Sky channels? Is the latest Kylie CD single with all the mixes really necessary or can you wait for her album? Do you really need the extra pair of trousers that are half price in the sale or are you buying them because they're cheap? If you master this thought process alone then half the battle is won.

When you go out – don't stay out late! I find that when I stay out later I spend more. More on drinks, food, taxis and club entrances. Go home early! I'm not saying just stay out for an hour or so but try to arrive early and go home early. You'll find out that you'll come home with some cash in your pocket rather than having to revisit the cash machines on the night out and regretting it later!

Look out for the deals bars, clubs, cinemas and restaurants are offering. The entertainment market is a highly competitive one. Virtually every evening spot has an offer going on. Take advantage of this! Look out for flyers or leaflets available at their premises. Scan the local press for a restaurant trying to drum up a bit more business. Pay close attention to the TV ads when Pizza Hut and others are doing a promotion.

v) Loans and savings plans

Switch credit cards and loans to obtain the best deals. 0% APR for balance transfers – sounds familiar? I'm sure you've heard this so many times that it no longer means anything – but it does! It means that you can save a lot of cash as you pay no interest on your borrowing. Make sure you capitalise on these deals to save you real money. But don't just be happy with saving money – make an effort to clear these balances! You will run out of credit companies eventually so you do need to clear this type of unhealthy borrowing.

Cash in or freeze payments to endowment policies and pension plans. Is the endowment policy you are contributing to really going to mature to its estimated value? You could cash it in, raise cash and save cash as you no longer need to contribute to it.

It's the same for pension contributions. You could freeze payments, which will result in an instant saving. When I used to work I was tempted to contribute to a pension. But after careful thought I realised that under no circumstances was I going to hand over any of my hard earned cash to a company that would 'play' with it on the stock market, be unsure of how much I would get back and never access until I was of retirement age.

3. Increase your income

I can already hear you – how do I increase my income? Well this depends on you. You need to be assertive, hard working and just that little bit cleverer than the rest! There are eight ways that I can think of that will instantly increase your income. This does assumes you have a job or a business in the first place:

■ work extra hours;
■ take on another job;
■ ask for a pay rise;
■ change your job;
■ claim all benefits due;
■ exchange benefits for cash;
■ switch from permanent employment to sub-contractor;
■ increase profitability.

See, I told you - it depends on you! Let's look at these ways in more detail.

How	Description
Work extra hours	Are there possibilities to do overtime, work weekends or do nightshift work and get paid for it? You'll probably find out that you will get in excess of your normal hourly rate but even if you don't – still do it! If it means you earn more money then it all goes into funding the shortfall. As long as the opportunity of overtime exists then do it and use it for either payment or time to do things that will either make or save you money.
Take on another job	Do you do a 9-5 office job and have your evenings free? I know people who work in pubs and nightclubs who have an office job in the day. It's a great way to increase your social circle. It also means you have less time to spend money as you are working! If you find a job that is a bit of fun then it will not seem that you are working day and night.

How	Description
	What about setting up another small business? If you're passionate about vintage clothes then why not start a market stall on a Saturday? If you're a DJ then go down to your local bars and nightclubs and try to get a spot. Even if you don't get paid you'll save on the perks you get like free drinks and entrance costs.
Ask for a pay rise	The reason why men get paid more than women is largely due to the fact that they ask for more! If you think you are worth more then go knock on your boss's office door and ask for a pay rise. Back your request up with what you have done for the company, market rate for your type of job and the loyalty you have shown to the business.
	I employ three people and I have one guy who frequently asks me for a pay rise – and I like that! He's hungry to prove himself so I promise to increase his pay based on results. He's had two pay rises already and he's only worked for me for eight months!
Change your job	This is an extreme measure but a valid one. There is no point staying in a job that's below your perceived market rate. It breeds resentment to your employer and it drains your energy and motivation.
	Put your feelers out. Let your friends and family know that you're looking. Scan the newspapers for the latest advertised jobs. Write to companies for which you would like

How	Description
	to work. Ring up the personnel department and tell them you want to work for them. So get your CV up to date and start making some moves!
Claim all benefits due	The government has a multitude of benefits to claim even if you are working. There is the family tax credit for starters. Families can have both adults working and still be eligible for some form of credit. There is about £1 billion worth of unclaimed benefits every year. You've seen the TV adverts – 'It's money with your name on it!'
Exchange benefits for cash	You may have a company car that you use. Employers offer cash alternatives instead of the car. You may find that you can run a car cheaper than the cash alternative, hence an instant saving and a positive effect on your income.
	Do you get any benefits from your employer that offer a cash alternative and you could provide to yourself cheaper than them? There's no point having a brand new car and struggling to meet the mortgage payment.
Switch from permanent employment to sub-contractor	Usually this happens the other way round. If you're a subcontractor earning £70,000 pa, and good at your job, the company may offer you full-time employment for £45,000 pa. For this you get job security and access to employer benefits such as their health and pension benefits. This is an expensive price to pay. In this example, which is a real example

How	Description
	as one of my good friends did this, you lose £25,000 for not much. Okay, he'll get a redundancy payment if made redundant but you have to evaluate how likely this is. It's worth asking your employer, if it is an environment for subcontractor work, to consider you switching to subcontractor income from salaried employment. The increase in pay could be quite staggering.
Increase profitability	This is a book in itself! For those of you who have a business you should always be looking at ways to increase profitability. Some obvious ways are: ■ Reducing the hours worked by your staff and doing the work yourself thus saving on wages and salary costs. ■ Pushing more sales through existing customers thus increasing turnover. ■ Advertising for more business thus increasing turnover. ■ Negotiating harder with your suppliers to reduce costs of sale. ■ Switching to banks which are offering lower costs of borrowings thus reducing bank and interest charges. Now it all depends on your business and how practical this is. But it is worth a think. Look over all the lines of your profit and loss account and see if you can either increase turnover or decrease expenditure or even both!

Ensure that if you are on a repayment mortgage then you switch to an interest only mortgage as this will lower the monthly payment quite dramatically. Now knowing how long you're going to have to fund this shortfall would be nice. What you want to know is how bad this cold spot is going to be and how long is it going to last. You need to be aware of certain key variables so you can gauge the likely damage of being in the cold spot environment. The following variables in the awareness table play a key part in determining how long and how bad the cold spot will be.

Awareness table

Global rates

Our rates are restricted partially by global rates. We cannot be out of sync with the rest of the world. This is called interest rate parity. The formula holds:

$$\frac{F}{S} = \left\{ \frac{1 + R_A}{1 + R_B} \right\}^T$$

Where **S** is the spot exchange rate, expressed as the price in currency **A** of one unit of currency **B**. **F** is the forward rate, R_A and R_B are the interest rates in the respective countries, and **T** is the common maturity for the forward rate and the two interest rates. This assumes that if interest rates were 10% in Europe then we would convert all our sterling to Euros, place them on deposit in a European bank and then convert them back after a year and enjoy the profit. This theory states that the profit would be nil as it would be money for nothing and so when you converted back in sterling you would get an inferior exchange rate. So we are all locked within each country's interest rate.

I am sure there are large banks exploiting this model and profiting from these imperfections within the market.

Home rates   Taking into account the interest rate parity above, there
will still however be some freedom within the UK to set
rates. The rate is set by the Bank of England under
licence from the government and they use the following
reports to set them:

- Consumer price index – this measures price inflation.
  The target for the bank is 2.5%. If it goes over that
  then it is expected the Bank will raise interest rates.
  Also a report needs to go to the government on why
  inflation rates have risen.
- Employment cost index – this measures wages growth.
  A rise in wages means more spending which means
  price inflation. Wage inflation is measured to try and
  predict forthcoming price inflation.
- GDP report – this measures the overall performance of
  our economy. Rates are dropped when the GDP drops
  for two consecutive quarters.
- Unemployment rate – unemployment needs to be
  within certain levels to keep consumer spending and
  thus prices down. Unemployment rates are used to try
  and predict future inflation rates.
- House price inflation – very under-rated by the Bank!
  They look at house price inflation and aim to use
  interest rates as a way of curbing prices but I've never
  seen the Bank Of England actually employing this
  tactic. We have seen massive gains over the last
  decade but the Bank needs to see extraordinary growth
  before these have an effect on interest rates.

It's very important to follow these indices which the
banks follows. It becomes very easy to predict which way
rates are going to go for the next three to six months.
Beyond that you are in the lap of the gods but this three
to six month window can give you the time to react to
the market and take drastic action – like sell!

| Negative equity | If people are in negative equity this leads to loss in the feel good factor. This reduces spending, which results in reduced prices, a lowering of GDP, job losses, recession and ultimately lower property prices. |

CHAPTER EIGHT

9pm to 12 midnight – Warm Spot

9pm...it's getting warm

So we have seen a rapid decline in property prices. Repossessions are higher than they've ever been in the last five years, negative equity has swamped the nation – who in the hell would want to get in to property investment? Well, to be frank – not a lot of people! Only people like me. Professional investors hate having money in the bank. There is absolutely no excitement in keeping your money in the bank. The return is guaranteed two things:

a) it's certain
b) it's low.

Basically it's certainly low! If you are a true business person you would never accept a low return on your money even if it was certain.

So amongst the carnage below that is happening within the property market the vultures, being the professional property investors, hover above waiting to swoop. The professional investor will know that it's a buyers' market rather than a sellers' market. They will accelerate the fall in prices as they know what price will put money in their pocket. So for example if they see a property advertised at £100,000 and know that the property is worth buying at £85,000, then considering it's a buyers' market they will simply place a cheeky offer of anywhere between £75,000 to £85,000. If the vendor is desperate to sell they will entertain this offer so as to limit the damage of holding this property.

9pm – 12 midnight

Interest rates have peaked. Property has got a bad name. Property investment is now considered a stupid thing to do. People who had bought properties to then sell, banking on historic growth rates, are now left with a hot potato. For the fortunate people who have money and who want to still speculate are heading towards their nearest stockbroker to play the stock market. The professional property investor however, never favouring the stock market, watches property prices on a daily basis to see when the price falls to a level that will put money in their pocket.

So who buys at 9pm? It's the professional property investor who will accept the lowest yield. In my experience the lowest yield will be a 2% loading on the current borrowing rate on the most desirable rental properties. So if the interest rate is 8% and buy to let mortgage rates are 9.5% then the lowest yield acceptable will be 11.5%, being 9.5% + 2%= 11.5%. Their reason for choosing the most desirable rental properties is because a 2% loading does not allow for too much void periods. Look at this example.

There are two properties for sale, with current rents and corresponding yields:

	Advertised price	Rent	Yield
An ex-local authority studio flat	£60,000	£6,000pa	10%
A private two-bed house	£100,000	£10,000pa	10%

Due to the yields being equal the professional investor will assess the likely voids of both properties. With the ex-local authority studio flat it will be likely that the tenant will out-grow the flat quickly as it is only a studio flat. Also, being an ex-local authority flat, it will only appeal to a limited audience. A two-bed private house will be a decent sized living space for a single person, couple or one child family and it will appeal to a wider audience due to it being in a private area. The investor will estimate that the voids will be longer with the ex-local authority studio flat compared to the two-bed private house.

However, the yield is below their target of 11.5%. They have to buy the property at:

$$\frac{\text{Annual rent}}{\text{Yield}} = \text{Property price} \qquad \frac{£10,000}{11.5\%} = £86,956$$

to ensure that they get a 11.5% yield. So the professional investor will go in with a bid of around £80,000 (as professional investors are cheeky and do not care if they offer 20% below what the vendor is asking!) and will happily negotiate at a price of around £87,000.

Sometimes vendors will accept less than £87,000 as they are desperate to sell thus pushing prices down further. So in the above example an offer of £80,000 might get accepted thus setting the new price levels for two-bed private houses.

Ex-local authority studio flats need to come down even further! As this is at the undesired end of the market professional investors may require a loading of 6%. If borrowing rates are 9.5% then a yield of 9.5% + 6% = 15.5% will be needed from the most cautious of investor! This equates to:

$$\frac{£6,000}{15.5\%} = £38,710$$

So a bid of £38,710 is all that the professional investor will pay. So prices have fallen further.

Now notice that I have not mentioned the owner-occupier in all of this. The owner-occupier does not operate to fundamentals. The owner-occupier will be solely focused on the property price itself. If they see prices falling then their worst fear is buying a property that immediately falls in value. The owner-occupier will wait until prices bottom out. The problem is the owner-occupier doesn't spend every day doing this like a professional investor! The professional investor does as it's their livelihood. The owner-occupier has other things to do – like their job!

Property prices will continue to be bid downwards, the best rental properties being bought first with the lower end rental properties having to fall further. New entrant professional investors will enter, with higher loadings on their requirements causing the prices to fall further but the lower end of the market just simply having to fall further to attract any interest. There comes a point, however, when prices at the lower end of the market catch the eye of one investor (someone like me!) who thinks – hang on a second, these properties are *cheap!* They start to buy where the market has bottomed out and as a result provide fantastic returns. So fantastic that other investors get wind of it and before you know it – the clock strikes 12 midnight!

So here we have the complete loop. As the clock strikes 12 midnight we are simply back to a hot spot. Then all the principles in Chapter 5 are applicable.

Looking at it as a sweeping hand of a clock:

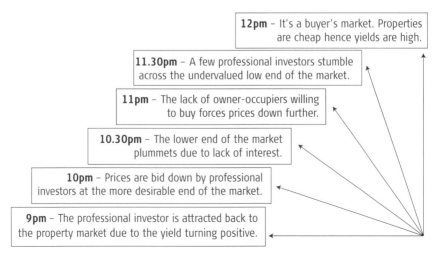

12pm – It's a buyer's market. Properties are cheap hence yields are high.

11.30pm – A few professional investors stumble across the undervalued low end of the market.

11pm – The lack of owner-occupiers willing to buy forces prices down further.

10.30pm – The lower end of the market plummets due to lack of interest.

10pm – Prices are bid down by professional investors at the more desirable end of the market.

9pm – The professional investor is attracted back to the property market due to the yield turning positive.

Strategies within a warm spot

The key strategy is to bid low. Do not be scared of insulting the vendor with your offer. An offer is an offer no matter what price you bid at. It's up to them to say yes or no. At least your offer is on the table for them to consider now. It may get rejected now but accepted a few weeks down the line. Do not wait for the prices to fall to your desired level – this is apathetic! It's up to you to drive the price down. If you simply wait it is likely that another investor will get there before you.

Making your offer stand out
If you're going to bid low, then make sure it's serious. Not seriously low but a serious offer worth considering. A vendor may accept a lower than anticipated offer if it is one of the following.

Type of offer	Description
A cash offer	This will mean that the sale, theoretically, will happen quickly as there is no mortgage to be obtained. This will mean no survey to highlight any potential problems with the property. If a vendor knows there will be no complications with regards to the finance then the vendor will favour this offer. Sometimes vendors favour a lower cash offer rather than a higher mortgage offer. It simply eliminates the lender from the transaction as we all know lenders can be awkward even at the best of times.
	To back up your cash offer show them your bank statement to prove you have the cash. This will really improve your chances of the vendor accepting your bid.

Type of offer	Description
Backed by a mortgage in principle	If you do not have nice tidy sum in your bank account to make a cash offer then get a mortgage in principle (MIP). This is where a lender has already credit checked you and has agreed to lend subject to the property only. This will send out the message to the vendor that you have already done the preliminaries to get the finance. All that is required is that the property gets valued up to the agreed price and the property is suitable security for mortgage purposes.
A flexible offer	Sometimes if you can be flexible in your offer this helps a lot. If the vendor says that they are happy to accept your price but wants to move out in six months' time and you are in no hurry to acquire the property then they are likely to consider your offer. Some vendors wish to take certain fixtures and fittings with them that the normal purchaser would not expect, like fancy doors or fireplaces. If you allow them to do this, stipulating that they replace or make good the damage they may cause as a result of taking these fixtures and fittings, then they may be more interested in your offer.

Financing

You may well find that obtaining finance in a falling market may not be that easy. This is because the banks would have got their fingers burnt due to defaulters in negative equity. Lending criteria will be stricter. They may require:

■ **A larger deposit** – to lower the risk to the lender. If, for example, they restrict lending to 50% loan to value then the property price will have to fall by 50% before the bank starts to get worried. This will be a big problem for you as you have to come up with the other 50%!

■ **Full status** – instead of the bank lending on the strength of the property to pay the mortgage they may look at the property and your status. They may ask that you earn in excess of £50,000pa and that you can prove it. This will mean payslips, tax assessments or certified accounts. Visit www.accdirect.co.uk

■ **A proven background** – as the banks become more cautious they may restrict lending to professional landlords only. This may be decided on how many years you have been in the business or how many properties you have got.

So to ensure that you are able to buy within a falling market you need:

■ **Cash** – for a deposit. More cash may be needed than expected. Ensure that you've remortgaged yourself to the hilt! This means that you will have the cash to put down. You do not want to be in the situation where you can get a flat for £25,000, that rents out for £500pcm (24% yield!) but you can't raise the 50% deposit (£12,500) from one of the few lenders still remaining in the buy to let market. Once the market recovers you will be able to re-access the £12,500 (and more!) put down as lenders warm back to the idea of buy to let. Once the flat recovers to £50,000 and lenders are willing to lend 85% loan to value then your £12,500 put down will raise an extra £30,000 to buy further properties ((£50,000 x 85%) – (£25,000 x 50%) = £30,000).

■ **Status** – make sure you can prove your income. If you are employed then be in a good job. If you are self-employed ensure that you have been so for three years and you have certified accounts.

■ **Experience** – make sure you've got a well performing portfolio under your belt. The threshold is usually around five properties and three years' experience. This will make you stand out from the rest.

CHAPTER NINE

Strategy Summary

Since I have dissected the property cycle into four distinct sections, let me put all four quadrants together so we all can understand it better.

As a result of the actions by us and others we can simplify the strategies within each spot *(see page 106-7)*.

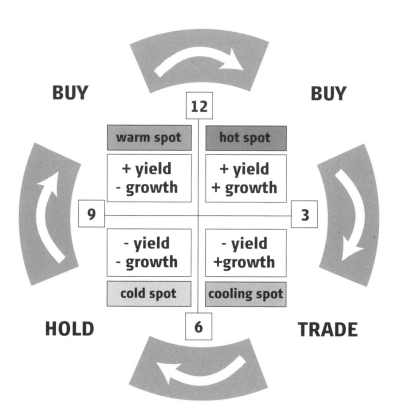

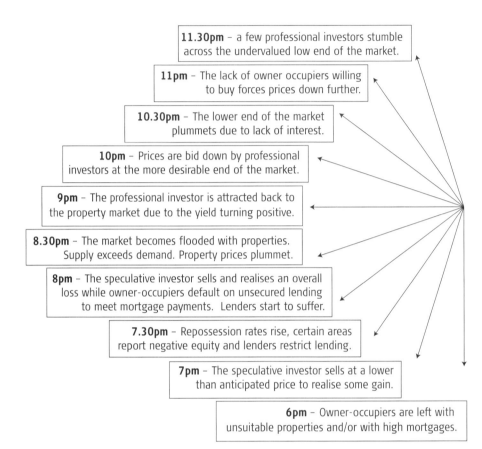

11.30pm – a few professional investors stumble across the undervalued low end of the market.

11pm – The lack of owner occupiers willing to buy forces prices down further.

10.30pm – The lower end of the market plummets due to lack of interest.

10pm – Prices are bid down by professional investors at the more desirable end of the market.

9pm – The professional investor is attracted back to the property market due to the yield turning positive.

8.30pm – The market becomes flooded with properties. Supply exceeds demand. Property prices plummet.

8pm – The speculative investor sells and realises an overall loss while owner-occupiers default on unsecured lending to meet mortgage payments. Lenders start to suffer.

7.30pm – Repossession rates rise, certain areas report negative equity and lenders restrict lending.

7pm – The speculative investor sells at a lower than anticipated price to realise some gain.

6pm – Owner-occupiers are left with unsuitable properties and/or with high mortgages.

So we can see that if you are a true professional investor you will only ever be interested in warm and hot spots. The reasons being:

■ **Hot spot** – you are prompted to buy. Buying is the only true way to participate in the property market. If the strategy was to sell then it is a sure way to get out of the property market. So finding hot spot areas is key if you want to grow within the property market.

■ **Cooling spot** – you are prompted to trade. Trading is buying and then selling. So in effect you dip in and out of the market. No professional investor would do this as it exposes you to massive

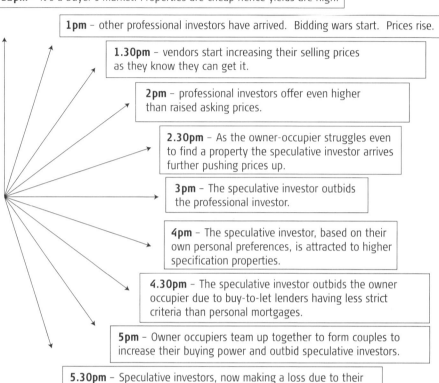

12pm – It's a buyer's market. Properties are cheap hence yields are high.

1pm – other professional investors have arrived. Bidding wars start. Prices rise.

1.30pm – vendors start increasing their selling prices as they know they can get it.

2pm – professional investors offer even higher than raised asking prices.

2.30pm – As the owner-occupier struggles even to find a property the speculative investor arrives further pushing prices up.

3pm – The speculative investor outbids the professional investor.

4pm – The speculative investor, based on their own personal preferences, is attracted to higher specification properties.

4.30pm – The speculative investor outbids the owner occupier due to buy-to-let lenders having less strict criteria than personal mortgages.

5pm – Owner occupiers team up together to form couples to increase their buying power and outbid speculative investors.

5.30pm – Speculative investors, now making a loss due to their miscalculations, sell to owner-occupiers and realise a capital gain.

gains as well as massive losses. Massive gains are acceptable (and well received!) but massive losses are possible and potentially bankruptable which is definitely unacceptable.

■ **Cold spot** – you are prompted to hold. How exciting is that! No buying or selling is required so no real strategy is required here.

■ **Warm spot** – you are prompted to buy. Again this is the only way to grow as you are prompted to buy just like a hot spot. If you can find a warm spot then it will only turn in to a hot spot so massive gains are inevitable.

So in a nutshell you should only ever be interested when an area is either a hot spot or a warm spot as it prompts you to buy. So how do you find both of these? Read on....

How to find a hot or warm spot

I have never found a warm spot in my time in property investment. I started property investment in 1996 so there has always been a hot spot to be found. The principles in finding a warm spot are the same as finding a hot spot. One should only ever seek a warm spot when there are no more hot spots. Currently there are hot spots in the UK, but there will be a time when there will be no hot spots and warm spots are the only places to invest.

The ways I have found hot spots are as follows.

Method	Description
Internet	The easiest way to travel the world without leaving your desk! I owe a substantial amount of my success to the internet as I was able to discover areas that I had never heard of. These unknown areas now form a significant part of my portfolio!
	I hope you would have gathered from reading this book that you have to find cheap properties. Generally it's properties under £60,000. All you do is visit these four sites:
	■ www.rightmove.co.uk ■ www.asserta.com
	■ www.vebra.com ■ www.home.co.uk.
	Type in any town or city you can think of and search the widest radius possible. Put in maximum price £60,000 and see what comes up! If nothing has come up then the town or city you entered is not a

Method	Description
	hot spot, nor any town surrounding. If something comes up then check it out further. If quite a few come up then bingo!
	Once you have found an area then visit www.ukpropertyshop.com. Here you have all the individual estate agents in that area. Check all their websites to see what they've got also. If it looks good then get in your car, drive down and buy everything you can!
Always look in agents' windows	If you visit an area then always check estate agents' windows. I do this out of habit and interest. I am interested in property even if it isn't going to make me any money. It's good to get an idea of property prices wherever you visit. You never know, you may stumble across a bargain.
Get the local press	Don't just stop at agents' windows. Get the local press and scan the property section. Here you can gauge the whole market in that area. You may find that there is an agent that specialises in low value properties.
Look for areas that are self-sufficient	Areas with bad transport links or that are a bit isolated make perfect hot spots. They are sometimes valued low due to lack of demand by buyers (because unless you work there, there is no point in living there) but have high tenant demand due to people wishing to rent there. One of my areas where I have a significant portfolio is Corby which meets this criteria. It has no train station, is 30 miles from anywhere significant but has a large Scottish community who wish to live there.

Method	Description
Get out there!	Go visit places. If you haven't seen a friend because they've moved to another area then go and see them! If you've always wondered what Stoke-on-Trent is like then take your other half and visit. Look at a map of the UK, pick an area that you like the sound of and go and visit it, stopping off at all the towns en route to check out the estate agents. See it as a mini adventure – go on, have some fun!

If all of that seems like hard work then visit my site, www.propertyhotspots.net, where you will find out all the hot spots that I could find and areas that are soon to be hot spots (and a hell of a lot more!).

CHAPTER TEN

Lifetime Property Clock

The property clock has a typical duration of anywhere between three and ten years. There are longer durations that exist, typically 40 years+, within our own home ownership goals. If we understand this cycle, which I call the lifetime property clock, we can then have a whole understanding of the property market. This is because the property market is made up of investors following the property clock and owner-occupiers following the lifetime property clock who look for a home to live and bring up their family in. Look at the following diagram:

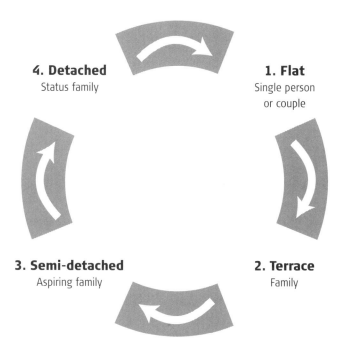

4. Detached
Status family

1. Flat
Single person
or couple

3. Semi-detached
Aspiring family

2. Terrace
Family

We can see that there is a definitive clock that exists within our own personal property goals over our lifetime. Let's look at the detail of each stage of the clock.

1. Single person or young couple aged 20 to 30

You start your working life, more specifically receiving a pay packet, and start spending what you earn on all sorts of products and services like clothes, electrical items, eating out etc. But you do all this from your parents' home! There then comes a point when you want your own place as it doesn't look that cool having the latest designer gear, the Porsche, but still living in your bedroom that you have been in since you were born! A 'pad' is needed to prove that you are independent. At this time the single person turns into a first-time buyer. There will be scenarios where a couple gets together to buy for the first time and they will also fit into this category.

First-time buyers (being single people and young couples) will want to preserve as much disposable income as possible. This is because it is the younger working generations that like to spend in the bars, clubs, restaurants, high streets and travel agents and they need the money to do so. So they will aim to buy a property that:

1. Is cheaper than paying rent.
2. Is not surplus to their needs.
3. Is easy to maintain.

The properties that meet this criteria will be at the cheaper end of the market. Specifically they will be studio, one and two-bed flats. Invariably these types of properties will be cheaper than the terraced, semis and detached properties. There will be exceptions to this rule. Consider the cost of riverside luxury apartments and penthouses compared with the cost of ex-local authority houses. The riverside flats will be more expensive than the terraced and semi-detached properties but it will be likely that the buyer of these flats will not be your typical buyer. It may be a second home for a wealthy businessman or a second or third-time buy by a young professional moving up the corporate ladder. It could be the case that the lifetime property clock for some individuals will only ever consist of flats but these cases will be rare and can be eliminated from this clock as we are dealing with the norms. They will also be smaller than all the other property types and maintained by someone else, typically the freeholder.

So first-time buyers will be drawn to flats. This can be seen by the way newly constructed flats are marketed. The show flat is decorated to a modern standard as the developer knows that the typical buyer of the flats will be young so they to make the show flat appeal to the young. Second bedrooms are dressed up as study rooms rather than baby rooms. Living rooms are larger at the expense of the kitchen as the developer knows that the young often eat out and prefer a larger living space.

So it is established that flats are typically bought by first-time buyers. I have assumed that a first-time buyer is *not* a young family. There may be some young families that do look to get on the property ladder but again, we are working within norms. An example of this would be Jack.

Jack has £8,000 saved and earns £18,000 per year. In his area he sees flats going for around £75,000 and houses going for £120,000 plus. His buying power is calculated as:

$$\text{Buying power} = (\text{deposit you actually have}) + (\text{mortgage you're able to get})$$

To calculate what he can afford we just plug in the figures. The deposit is £8,000 and the mortgage he is able to get will be four times his salary. So buying power is calculated as:

$$\text{Buying power} = £8,000 + (4 \times £18,000)$$

Which equates to £80,000. So we can see he can clearly only afford a flat. So he buys a nice one-bed flat near the town for £80,000.

So as nature follows its natural course what happens next to the first-time buyer is:

- if it's a single person they meet the love of their life and decide to have a family;
- if it's a couple they decide to have a family.

It becomes apparent that having your children sleep in the same room as you do is not such a good idea! A bigger property is required, preferably with a garden for the child or children to play in. Therefore a house is needed…

2. Family aged 30 to 40

It is probable that two things would have happened to the first-time buyer in the time since moving.

1. **Equity increase.** The flat that the first-time buyer owns would have grown in value. This would mean that instead of the mortgage balance being around 90% of the value of the home the balance will be somewhere around 40-80% of the value depending on timing and how the market has performed. There may be a situation where the mortgage balance is greater than the property value (called negative equity) but if this situation has occurred the couple simply have to wait it out until prices recover so that they can move. Therefore people in this situation cannot be second-time buyers as they are stuck in their homes unable to participate in the market.

2. **Salary increase.** It is likely that the first-time buyer's salary would have increased due to promotion, career progression etc. This means that the first-time buyer can borrow more to acquire their second property.

Due to both of these things happening the first-time buyer can buy a better property – a house! This is because they now have a larger deposit due to an increase in equity and increased borrowing power due to an increase in salary. Using the same example above let's say Jack, five years down the line, meets Jill (who also owns her flat and bought at the same time), his next door neighbour, and they get married and decide to plan a family. They decide to sell both their flats, use the equity and combine their salaries to buy a nice three-bed terrace property in the same town.

	Jack	Jill	Total
Value of flat	£100,000	£100,000	£200,000
Mortgage balance	£72,000	£72,000	£144,000
Equity	£28,000	£28,000	£56,000
Salary	£23,000	£23,000	£46,000

So their buying power follows the same equation:

Buying power = (deposit you actually have)
+ (mortgage you're able to get)

The deposit is £56,000 and the mortgage they will be able to get will be 2.75 times joint salary. So buying power is calculated as:

Buying power = £56,000 + (2.75 x £46,000)

Which equates to £182,500. So Jack and Jill buy the nice three-bed terrace that they had their eye on for £182,500 and start a family.

The majority of the population will stop here. The second-time buy house will meet all their basic needs like a room for each child, space for a decent dining table, garden etc. The aims for the family will be to clear the mortgage by the time they hit retirement age or before. The only time a second-time buyer becomes a third-time buyer is when one of these happens.

1. **Another child.** The household outgrows the house due to the arrival of another child.

2. **Income.** The household income increases significantly due to one or both members rising up the corporate ladder in their professional job or if one of the members runs their own business and it does well. The household will seek a better house as they can afford it.

3. **Inheritance.** The household receives an inheritance which is significant enough to invest into their property aspirations.

In the first instance, where the family outgrows the house, the household income would not have changed so the household can only afford the house that they currently live in. In order to move to a house of the same value, but larger, the household may forgo such benefits of the original house as proximity to the town centre, train station or quality of area to obtain the larger house. This type of third-time buyer will buy another terraced house with simply more bedrooms for the same price, like moving from a three-bed private terrace to a four-bed ex-local authority house. So here there is no progression in price. It's more like a sideways move within the lifetime property clock.

In the second and third instance there is a progression in price. A higher value property is sought. This is a valid third-time buyer as they are moving upwards in the property market. This is what I call the aspiring family.

3. Aspiring family aged 35 to 55

The two scenarios where a household is able to move up the property ladder are when their buying power increases further. Looking at the buying power equation and seeing where each situation occurs shows the following:

Buying power = (deposit you actually have) + (mortgage you're able to get)

Inheritance - The household receives an inheritance which is significant enough to invest in their property aspirations. This increases the deposit and therefore their buying power.

Income - The household income increases significantly due to one or both members rising up the corporate ladder in their professional job or if one of the members runs their own business and does well. The household will seek a better house as they can afford it. This increases their borrowing power as their combined salary is higher.

So using the same example, suppose Jack and Jill were to make consultant level at their office jobs with an 80% increase in their salary then their individual pay will go from £23,000 to £41,400. Then the mortgage they are able to get increases from:

2.75 x (£23,000 + £23,000) = £126,500

to

2.75 x (£41,400 + £41,400) = £227,700

That's an increase of £227,700 - £126,500 = £ 101,200.

So now Jack and Jill can look at a house, assuming property prices have remained at the same level, for £101,200 more than their house is worth, which equates to £182,500 + £101,200 = £283,700. This will probably buy them a nice four-bed semi or three-bed detached in a private area. The same house could be bought if there was no increase in salary but Jack's remaining parent left £101,200 on their death.

Most third-time buyers will stop here. It will be a quiet and safe enough area to enjoy a happy life for them and their children. The only family left looking to move again is the Status Family…

4. Status family aged 40 to 60

So what makes someone want to buy for the fourth time? Status! If the property they live in is meeting all their needs then the mind slowly turns 'wants' in to 'needs'. Like:

I *need* a triple garage to house my three cars as they might get stolen.
I *need* a swimming pool and gym to keep fit for my health.
I *need* a large garden so my children can play safely.
I *need* a separate study room as it will better my ability to work.

I am guilty of this! I want a house with a triple garage, swimming pool, large garden and separate office. I have convinced myself I need it but if I'm honest with myself I don't really need any of this. I am a single man and all I need is a one-bed flat. However, it hasn't stopped me looking for this type of property as I believe my life will be better if I do find one.

The buying power will be calculated the same as above. The figures can be anything as houses at this end of the market can range from £500,000 to £10m. There are very few executive houses relative to the number of other houses and the worth of these houses will be determined by very different fundamentals. Where the value of a three-bed terrace will be comparable with another three-bed terrace in the same street, and there will be plenty of buyers, executive homes have no comparables and very few buyers. Values of executive homes will be set by holding out for a buyer to fall in love with the house.

Take for example an executive home on the market for £1m. How many buyers do you think there are able to buy this home? Very few – that's for sure! The potential buyer will have to love the area, layout, space, style and much more if they are going to part with a large sum of money like a million pounds. So the vendor simply has to wait. If the vendor is in a hurry to sell they have to either drop their price to attract more potential buyers or improve the property's finish, but you find at the top end that few vendors require a quick sale.

It can be assumed that once someone is over 60 years of age they will be unlikely to want to move upwards in the property market. If anything, once a spouse dies, the remaining spouse leaves the home to move into a serviced retirement flat. So in effect they move round to position one again of being the single person.

Forced moves

I have ignored forced moves. That is to say moving house due to job relocation, divorce or sizing down. This is to keep the model simple. All these forced moves have an impact on the market but it is safe to say that people strive to move round the lifetime property clock in a clockwise fashion.

CHAPTER ELEVEN

Interaction Between the Property Clock and the Lifetime Property Clock

Since we are interested in property investment we must see how the property clock is relevant to the lifetime property clock. It's quite safe to say that the home ownership and rental sector will be made of properties in stages one and two and the home ownership sector only will be made up of properties in stages three and four. Looking at it diagrammatically:

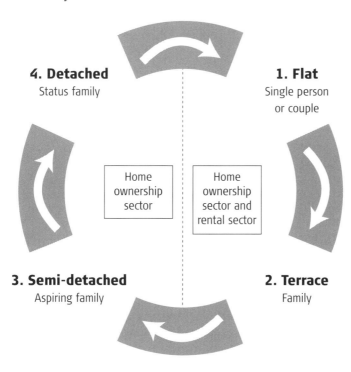

4. Detached
Status family

1. Flat
Single person
or couple

Home
ownership
sector

Home
ownership
sector and
rental sector

3. Semi-detached
Aspiring family

2. Terrace
Family

Just check out the rental lists of letting agents. They will predominately be for flats and terraced houses. There will be a few semis and detached houses available for rent but 90% or more will be the standard properties such as flats or terraced housing. There are two reasons for this.

1. Semis and detached houses are sold at a premium compared with a terraced property with the same number of bedrooms. However, the rent achievable for a semi or detached house will not compensate for the premium paid. This lowers the overall yield of the property hence making it unprofitable. Professional investors will shy away from such investments.

2. The only people able to afford such homes are people on their third-time buy. The price of semis and detached houses will be set by the gains made on their original property ladder climb so it will price out a lot of speculative investors also. Speculative investors would like to buy these properties as they will let out easily and are properties they feel comfortable with, but they will be out of their reach due to the high price these properties command.

Direct interaction

Since investors can only enter into stages one and two we can say that property investment directly interacts with stages one and two. Stages one and two involve the:

- young single person
- young couple
- young family

i.e. first-time buyers.

Property investment used to meet the need of people who had no interest in buying and hence would rent the properties bought by property investors quite happily. In other words we were in equilibrium between first-time buyers and investors. First-time buyers were able to buy as well as investors. Now what is happening is that investors are buying properties that are suitable for first-time buyers at a faster rate than first-time buyers, thus forcing them to rent rather than to buy the properties. What then happens is that the rental sector grows and the home ownership sector shrinks within stages one and two. If the home ownership sector shrinks too small it will affect stages three and four as there will be fewer buyers moving round the lifetime property clock. This will be the indirect interaction.

Indirect interaction

The best way to understand this is to look at extremes. So in the extreme, if stages one and two was at a ratio of 100% rental and 0% home ownership then the prices of semis and detached would have to fall as no one would have a gain on their previous property to put down as a deposit. This will slowly drive the prices of executive homes down as there will be no one to buy them. The prices will fall to a level just above the undifferentiated terraced properties.

So the mix of investors to first-time buyers is critical to sustain the prices of stages three and four. It is not, however, critical to prevent a crash in housing. You may read a lot about the lack of first-time buyers entering the market and that somehow it's going to trigger a crash, but this is a red herring. It will only cause ridiculously priced houses at the top end of the market to come back down to a sensible level.

Strategies

I love to go where no one else goes! This is the way you make serious money. So as everyone talks about the lack of first-time buyers and how they are priced out of the entry level of the market – you're looking at the other end! Check out how fast the semis and detached end is falling. At the moment I have found nothing but that doesn't mean there isn't anything out there. 'He who seeks will find.' One of my long-term plans is to cash in my whole lower end portfolio and buy fewer top end properties as a nice pension policy. Now I say long-term but if the semis and detached end starts yielding gross at 8 or 9% in a few years then this could be the way to go.

Look at this example, which is actually my real case:

Number of properties:	100
Property value:	£6m
Debt value:	£3.5m
Annual rent:	£420,000
Annual profit before tax:	£180,000

Let's say I sell my whole portfolio. I would net:

$$£6m - £3.5m = £2.5m$$

being the property value – debt value = net proceeds

Now if I could get 9% on this £2.5m from buying ten £250,000 higher end properties then my profit and loss account would look like this:

Rent (9% x £250,000)	£225,000
Mortgage cost (no borrowings)	£nil
Other costs (management, voids etc)	£45,000
Annual profit before tax:	£180,000

Spot the difference? Well, there is none! I would earn exactly the same as I would before. However, it would be a manageable portfolio since it is only ten properties, with a better class of tenant since they are higher end properties, hence less bad debt and lower maintenance due to being simply a smaller portfolio (fewer gas safety checks, actual floor space area etc).

There are two problems currently in achieving this:

1. I cannot find any 9% yielding higher end properties.
2. I would get clobbered with a large capital gains tax bill which is difficult to shelter.

These problems can be overcome. Firstly 9% yielding higher end properties will be available in times to come so it's simply a waiting game. Secondly the large tax bill can be treated as an expense and factored in so that you adjust the selling price to cover this cost. I am sure I will find a landlord who will buy my portfolio at my price when this time comes.

Good luck

Property is essentially a simple game if you understand a few fundamentals. The key is to buy when it puts money in your pocket and if possible increases your wealth. I know you've heard this time and time again but property is a long-term investment. If you treat it as such then you are on the long-term path to property millionairedom. I wish you luck with all your future property purchases and I hope you bear in mind the property clock.

Ajay Ahuja

Index

Other books by Ajay Ahuja

How to Get on the Property Ladder
The first-time buyer's guide to escaping the rent trap and owning your own home

You, Property and Your Pension
Using bricks and mortar as the safe route to a secure retirement

How to Make a Fortune on the Internet
A guide for enyone who wants to create a massive – and passive – income
for life

Investing in Student Buy-to-Let
How to make money from student accommodation

Property Hotspots Around the World
Find the best places to invest outside the UK

Other Services

The author also offers a portfolio-building service to clients of all sizes. He will help with:

◆ Sourcing the right properties tailored to your own investment strategy.
◆ Raising the cheapest finance to purchase the properties.
◆ Finding the right tenants.
◆ The ongoing maintenance of the properties.

If you are thinking of building a portfolio or need help expanding your portfolio then contact:

Ajay Ahuja ACA
Accountants Direct
99 Moreton Road
Ongar
Essex
CM3 0AR

Tel: 0800 652 3979
Fax: 01277 362563
Email: emergencyaccountants@yahoo.co.uk
www.buytolethotspots.com

fastlet.com
The author offers a fixed price buy-to-let refurbishment service. It includes a new kitchen & bathroom and starts from £5250 inclusive of VAT for a studio flat. It is a national service and completion dates are from 21 days from instruction. £100 per day penalties are payable by fastlet.com if they complete the project late. Contact author above.

If you want to know how...

- To buy a home in the sun, and let it out
- To move overseas, and work well with the people who live there
- To get the job you want, in the career you like
- To plan a wedding, and make the Best Man`s speech
- To build your own home, or manage a conversion
- To buy and sell houses, and make money from doing so
- To gain new skills and learning, at a later time in life
- To empower yourself, and improve your lifestyle
- To start your own business, and run it profitably
- To prepare for your retirement, and generate a pension
- To improve your English, or write a PhD
- To be a more effective manager, and a good communicator
- To write a book, and get it published

If you want to know how to do all these things and much, much more…

howtobooks

If you want to know how ...
to make your first property
purchase a success

The Beginner's Guide to Property Investment

The ultimate handbook for first-time buyers and would-be property investors

Tony Booth

This book provides an insight into many key issues; it explains what constitutes a sound investment, how you can examine your borrowing potential and create a golden credit rating, what mortgages are available and which are most suitable. It also discusses alternative property investment; buy-to-let, let-to-buy, renovation, buying property abroad, self-build and self-employed business enterprise; and shares generous amounts of inside information and well-kept trade secrets.

'The sense of achievement gained from buying a first property is tremendous. It is a momentous occasion, filled with pride and contentment.

'It is true that there is a growing trend and an ever expanding ability to buy property, but there is associated with it a mountainous capacity for critical mistakes. This book is intended for savvy investors who wish to evade such errors. By following the advice laid out in this book, conducting a thorough personal assessment, investigating properties worthy of purchase and exploring all the alternatives, you will find yourself able to buy a dwelling that meets your needs and one that provides financial security for the future.' – **Tony Booth**

ISBN 978-1-85703-961-0

If you want to know how ... to build a property portfolio

How to be a Property Millionaire

From Coronation Street to Canary Wharf

Annie Hulley

TV star Annie Hulley has amassed a substantial property portfolio in just three years. In this book she explains how she achieved it, the mistakes she made along the way, and what she's gleaned from the experience.

'I now have a substantial investment property portfolio and that is the reason for writing this book, to show that from humble beginnings you too can achieve your goal of being a property millionaire.' – Annie Hulley

'A must-read book…a practical guide for anyone who has an interest in investing in bricks and mortar.' – OPP

'…loads of advice on getting on the property ladder in the UK, plus a section on holiday lets and second homes…and a chapter with advice on buying in foreign markets.' – Homes Worldwide

'Hulley's guide covers a huge range of subjects relating to buying property, including different types of mortgages, buying at auctions, buying off plan, tax liabilities, estate agents, holiday homes and much more. She's done her homework.' – Observer

ISBN 978-1-85703-857-6

If you want to know how ...
to build your own home

How to Build Your Own Home

The ultimate guide to managing a self-build project and creating your dream house

Tony Booth and Mike Dyson

More and more people are setting out to build their own dream home. This book will help you turn your dream into reality by explaining the process, stage-by-stage.

"Here you will find the practical knowledge required to go beyond your aspirations, to take that first step and start building the perfect home. At the end of the day, you will acquire the home you want, rather than one forced upon you from a limited variety, designed and constructed by a builder whose only motivation is to profit from your purchase. Instead of having to fit into a house, you can finally make a house fit you!"
Tony Booth and Mike Dyson

This book will guide you through the fundamental elements of the self-build programme, from identifying and assessing a suitable building-plot to arranging finance and contractors. It deals with architects and designers, surveyors, labourers and tradesmen. It explains how to obtain planning permission and where to find appropriate insurance protection whilst construction is underway. Essentially, this book provides you with the know-how you need to complete a successful self-build project.

ISBN 978-1-84528-192-2

If you want to know how ...
to build or renovate your home

Getting the Builders in

A step-by-step guide to supervising your own building projects

Leonard Sales

Aimed at the lay client, this book gives practical step-by-step insight on matters that even experts in this field frequently fail to appreciate. Project management is partly about methodology and partly common sense. This straightforward guide is a refreshing approach to a diverse subject and keeps both of these factors in perspective.

Author Leonard Sales, who has been in the construction industry for 26 years, has learned from experience that the clients who demand the highest standards and who are willing to work in conjunction with the contractor are the ones who generally get their projects finished on time and to budget. The book includes simple-to-use management techniques that the author has himself used successfully, and that would suit projects with values ranging from one thousand to one million pounds.

ISBN 978-1-84528-233-2

If you want to know how ...
to be a great landlord

The Landlord's Survival Guide

The only practical insiders' handbook for all privare landlords

Lesley Henderson

This concise but comprehensive guide is for first time – as well as established – landlords.

It is divided into sections, each of which is jam-packed with detail and insider tips. Most sections will only take minutes to read (although a few earlier ones take a little more) and each section tells you exactly what you need to do – and why – to get best results.

Each section has tips, skills, time management ideas, and problem solving advice, plus supportive guidance and helpful websites and phone numbers.

If you're looking for a bit of straight talking about your investment, or you're sufficiently interested to discover how to increase your own bottom line rather than some agent's, then this is the guide for you.

ISBN 978-1-84528-224-0

If you want to know how ...
to rent a house and keep smiling

The Tenant's Survival Guide

Essential reading for every tenant – and those who are planning to rent

Lesley Henderson

"If you're renting property make this book your bible." – Sunday Mirror

The Tenant's Survival Guide is the definitive guide to renting accommodation, containing clear and concise information unobtainaible from any other single source. It includes:

– What to look for during viewings
– How to protect your deposit
– Inventories – the practical essentials
– What happens if you decide to leave or the landlord gives you notice to quit
– Checklist of essentials
– Useful standard letters
– How to live within the legally defined terms of the contract

With rental payments consuming on average over one third of your disposable income – or closer to half for students – it's important to ensure your interests are safeguarded. If you are about to be a tenant, or are one already, you do need this book.

"A must for anyone renting property." – London Evening Standard

"The anecdotes had me howling with laughter." – Daily Telegraph

"Landlords will certainly pick up a few tips that will make you a better landlord." – Small Landlords Association

ISBN 978-1-84528-231-8

If you want to know how ...
to build a stock market portfolio

Investing in Stocks and Shares

A step-by-step guide to making money on the stock market

Dr John White

This book explains in plain English all there is to know about what affects share prices, how to avoid unnecessary risks and how to trade on the stock market, whether it's up or down.

'Will be a help to private investors…Gives an easy-to-understand guide to the way the stock market works, and how the investor should go about setting up a suitable investment strategy.' – What Investment

'If you have got money to spare, start by investing in the purchase of this book.' – Making Money

'User-friendly… Contains practical examples and illustrations of typical share-dealing documents…demystifies the world of stocks and shares.' – OwnBase

ISBN 978-184528-221-9

howto**books**

How To Books are available through all good bookshops, or you can order direct from us through Grantham Book Services.

Tel: +44 (0)1476 541080
Fax: +44 (0)1476 541061
Email: orders@gbs.tbs-ltd.co.uk

Or via our website: www.howtobooks.co.uk

To order via any of these methods please quote the title(s) of the book(s) and your credit card number together with its expiry date.

For further information about our books and catalogue, please contact:

How To Books
Spring Hill House
Spring Hill Road
Begbroke
Oxford
OX5 1RX

Visit our web site at www.howtobooks.co.uk

Or you can contact us by email at info@howtobooks.co.uk